Intr

The Art of Silence

By Dan Smith and Katherine Smith

Table of Contents

Introduction

I want to thank you and congratulate you for downloading the book, *"The Introvert: The Art of Silence"*.

When I was a little girl all grown-ups around me behaved a bit worried because of my timidity and because I was always "in my world." As I grew, my embarrassment when I was in the company of unknown or less known people grew with me. I was feeling rather good, but the people around me were trying to convince me that I was not well. In fact, they have always shared tips with me on how to be polite, and how to communicate with people even though I felt that I am not doing anything wrong, for example, I was never impertinent or arrogant as some other children. All this led to my conclusion that there is something wrong with me. Something must be wrong with thirteen year old girl that read a novel of thousand pages in two days.

My love for books led me into a position to be a school teacher. That's when I first realized the difference between introverts and extroverts, and that I belong to the first group. It was very difficult at the beginning to do a job that required constant attention and interaction, so I often wanted to give up that job, but my love for children didn't allow me to do that. Through a job as a teacher I have learned how difficult it is to be introvert in an extroverted world, but I have learned and how I can work on my communication skills, as well as how to develop the courage to improve my life experiences.

In the book " The Introvert: The Art of Silence" I presented my observations, as well as scientific observations of introverted people and children and how they can improve their self-esteem, make friends, flirt and improve their love life as well as other important relationships in their life. I hope you will learn a lot from this book on introverted people and I hope you will enjoy while learning.

Thanks again for downloading this book, I hope you enjoy it!

Chapter 1:
How to develop communication skills

1.1. Jung's distinction between introverts and extroverts

Let us first determine how feels and acts someone who can be defined as an introvert person. The first attributes that come to our mind when a word 'introvert' is spoken are uncommunicativeness, restraint and oversensitivity. These attributes are, of course, based on research of personality types and their characteristics. One of the greatest minds of psychoanalyzing, Karl Gustav Jung, the Swiss psychoanalyst, first made a distinction between introverts and extroverts. Here is what he thought were the characteristics of introverts versus extroverts.

Jung's analysis of extroverted and introverted is widely accepted, although not fully understood. Jung distinguishes two different attitudes towards life and, in that meaning, two models of behavior. These two different reactions to the circumstances are strong enough to be seen and described as typical. So, an extrovert person is characterized by an interest in people and things around him, the productive relationships with others and addiction of other people's opinion. This personality type is, by Jung, motivated by external factors and influences from the environment. Extroverts are social and feel safe even in a foreign environment. Such people have a good relationship with others even when they do not agree. Instead of withdrawal (which the opposite type tends to do), they are rather arguing or debating and trying to overturn everything in accordance with their own forms or needs.

Introverted, however, feel best when they are alone or when in a small intimate group. In conversation, they give preference to their own opinion than the generally accepted one. Someone, who is introverted, will leave for later to read a book that is popular or will diminish the value of something that is widely accepted. This independence of judgment and lack of conventionality are often a source of prejudice towards introverted people. I assume that most of you who read this book would like to belong to an extroverted type because you might believe that such people are more successful and happier. This book exactly wants to show and prove what the hidden powers of introverted people are as they are always in some way in modern society valued lower than extroverted.

The present system of socialization is far more adapted to extroverted persons, while the second type of people tends to be forgotten. Withdrawn people in this regard are harder to understand because their energy isn't focused on impressing others. Surely you have noticed while watching acquaintances that some of them have talent or knowledge of something rare, but don't like to be exposed. They are hard to persuade to demonstrate or express some of their amazing reflections in public, so you'll need plenty of time to get used to them and accept such a person.

People often have prejudices about things and people they do not understand. How introverted people are less accessible than extroverts, therefore, there are more unknowns that are the basis for prejudice. Let's review the 10 most common misconceptions and myths regarding introverted people.

Prejudices are negative judgments or opinions about a person, group or appearance created before the real, direct experience with that person, group or idea, or without the knowledge or researching facts about it. Also, in the narrow sense, prejudices are related to the irrational suspicion or hatred of a particular group of people, nation, race or religion. Prejudice is often based on social stereotypes, and in the most extreme variants is resulting in that a certain group of people abolishes human rights, or to some other group gives an unfair advantage. That's how the prejudice in any form is harmful to humans.

Myth # 1 - introverted people do not like to talk.

This is not true, introverted people just do not like to talk unless they have something to say, that is they do not like to chat. If you come up with a topic which is interesting to them, they will not stop talking for days. Introverts are just feeling dull when they have to talk about something that really doesn't interests them, that's all.

Myth # 2 - introverted people are shy.

Shyness has nothing to do with introversion. It does not mean that introverts are afraid of people. They just need a good reason to interact with others. If you want to talk to an introverted person, just start talking. Do not worry too much about whether you're too kind or not. The other thing is that they can become shy because sometimes even their near environment doesn't understand them.

Myth # 3 - introverted people are rude.

Introverted people often do not see the reason to be what they are not because social norms require so. They want everyone to be realistic and honest. Unfortunately, this behavior is not acceptable in most environments, so introverts can feel a lot of pressure to fit in, what is very exhausting for them. So, keep in mind that introverted people can become rude when you put a pressure on them to become something they are not because that frustrates them a lot.

Myth # 4 - Introverts do not like people.

On the contrary, introverts greatly appreciate their friends and people in general. They can count their close friends on the fingers of one hand. If you are lucky to have an introvert as a friend, you will probably have a faithful ally until the end of your life. My best friendships are from childhood and I am proud about it.

Myth # 5 - Introverts do not like to go out.

Nonsense! Introverts just do not like to spend much time in public. They absorb information and experiences quickly and, therefore, they do not have to stay long in a certain environment to understand it. They are ready to go home, recharge their batteries and process all that information. In fact, the "recharging the batteries" is of great importance to introverted people. I think it is of most importance that others understand this and not to have some sort of prejudices about this behavior of introverted people.

Myth # 6 - introverted people always want to be alone.

Introverted people feel quite well with their thoughts. They think and daydream a lot. They like to have the problems on which to work on and puzzles that can be solved. But they can also be very lonely if they do not have anyone to share their discoveries. They need a reliable and honest connection with one person at a time. Introverts can pay full attention only on one person at a time but that is what makes them good friends.

Myth # 7 - introverted people are strange.

Introverted people are often loners. They do not go after everything like most of the people. They prefer to be respected for their unusual lifestyle. They think for themselves and, therefore, are often at odds with the environment. Introverted people do not make decisions based on what is popular or trendy. Here is another prejudice of something we are not very familiar with. In my experience, I do not like to be alone, but when there isn't a person that suits me I would rather be alone.

Myth # 8 - introverts are withdrawn nerds.

Introverts are people who are primarily for themselves and pay the most attention to their own thoughts and emotions. Not that they are not able to pay attention to what is going on around them, but they find their inner world more interesting.

Myth # 9 - Introverts do not know how to relax and entertain.

Introverts are often relaxing at home or in nature, and not in the dynamic public places. Introverts are not looking for excitement and adrenaline. If there is too much noise, they would rather go home. I think that most of my close friend would not agree on that in any way since we always have a lot of fun when we are together.

Myth # 10 - Introverts can change and become extroverts.

Introverts cannot be changed and they deserve respect for their natural temperament and contributions to humankind. In fact, one study showed that the percentage of introverted people increases with IQ. I don't really know why they have to change anyway, but I do believe that they should work on their communication skill first.

We are all very well aware that the developed skills of social communication are in today's world highly desirable. If you establish contacts with people and maintain communication easily, you will be fancied, both among friends and colleagues, and possibly with the opposite sex as well. Introverted people have troubles to establish communication because they are ashamed to initiate the first contact. Besides, they are usually afraid that the person they want to talk will in some way refuse them, be rude or even mock at them. For these people, the social situations are more or less threatening place, from which they would prefer to run away or hide.

1.2. Are the skills of social communication innate?

The word skills mean that this is something that can be learned. It is also important to know that extraversion and introversion are two extreme poles of the same dimension or personality traits (Extraversion), so one can be closer to one pole or another. Most people balance between these two poles. The personality trait is something that is said to be predominantly a man's innate quality, and it is a predisposition that comes with birth.

If someone is extrovert by nature, he tends to communicate with as many people as possible and looks for excitement in every area of life. Unlike extrovert, introvert people communicate less when they are with people they do not know or are not close to them. It is more difficult for introverts to establish contacts and they often socialize only with a certain group of people. But, whether something can be changed? What happens when a person who is introverted by nature wants to become communicative?

Social communication skills can be learned! Thus, it is possible if you are by nature withdrawn to become more open and communicative. It is important to know that someone who is introvert by nature cannot become extrovert, but why should he anyway? It is enough to know that you can become more successful in social communication than you were before. You cannot be what you're not, but you can develop certain skills to the extent when it will become functional in everyday life. Therefore, do not despair and to think, "I'm not such a person, I will never succeed" because it is not true. What is true is that you are as you are, and if you want, you can change certain aspects of your behavior to have better outcomes.

1.3. Accept yourself as you are

The title of this part of the book may seem contrary to what has been said about that we can make changes. However, accepting yourself with feelings and behaviors that you have at this point is, in fact, the basis for a change for the better. It is generally known that if someone does not accept himself the way he is, he consumes a lot of energy on criticizing his own thoughts and behavior. Of course, this is the wrong path that does not lead to positive change we all desire. When you are truly reconciled with yourself, you will be more relaxed, authentic and open to learning new things, including social skills.

I can hear you wondering whether social skills can really be learned or it will all look awkward and you will seem even more ridiculous to yourself. These last two words are crucial because it is the low opinion you have about yourself that causes failures, including communication failures. Do you really think that others spend a lot of time thinking about your behavior? Well, no, they don't. They try to live as best as they can. Some want to improve their life experience, like you, who are reading this book, while others remain willfully trapped in some form of negative experience. So, first and foremost rule is: I accept myself so I could be open to learning.

Why do I insist on you accepting yourself that much? Because, I have introvert traits in my character and I always thought there was something wrong with me. I always questioned, criticized and rejected myself, until I found the gift. And that gift for me was acceptance. Maybe it will look naive for you to think that if you truly accept yourself, others will too. But, that is just what happened to me so I'm speaking from my own experience. I manage to accept myself through meditation, maybe you will find your individual path, but the outcome is the same and that is feeling more comfortable in your own skin. After accepting that you do not accept yourself, you can learn how to change and grow. Let's see what tips are given by the experts on how to improve your communication skills.

Introversion and acceptance

Understanding your introversion is closely associated with accepting yourself. My personal opinion is that is much harder for an introvert to accept himself in the world where extroversion is at a much higher price. In fact, I think the only way to true happiness leads through absolute acceptance of what we feel.

When we talk about acceptance of ourselves, one of the biggest challenges is acceptance of our emotional state. It is easy to accept yourself when you are satisfied, cheerful and calm. But what happens when you feel different? Through family and social heritage, we have acquired the habit of rejecting and ignoring our negative feelings. Surely you remember or you have seen how parents tell their children, "You're ugly when you cry," or send similar messages practically prohibiting negative feelings. Parents unwittingly tell the children they are bad if they exhibit anger, rage, sadness, and generally any feeling that is not affirmative. That's why we refuse to be sad, angry or cramped even before ourselves. We tend to reject these parts of ourselves, even though these "parts of us" have the greatest desire to be accepted.

In today's society to be happy is a question of prestige. It is part of the lifestyle that can be seen and the rest is hidden. To accept ourselves when we are not smiling and friendly is something illogical, it "makes no sense", what can we do with it? It is quite clear that these "bad" or difficult feelings dwell within us and we experience them as foreign objects. It seems that it is logical to try to avoid them. Those of you who have read the novel Stranger by Albert Camus know what I'm talking about.

By rejecting bad feelings within, we create the split that causes even more pain. Only when we embrace bad feelings, we can revive something. We can learn much more from "bad" feelings than the good ones. We very often grow spiritually and develop thanks to the bad feelings. The bad feelings of dissatisfaction force us to fight, to become stronger and develop new ways of overcoming obstacles. "Trigger" for the flotation of unwanted emotional state may be a minor reminiscent of the painful experiences of the past. For example, the disregard by the chief can draw out the repressed shame or sadness related to the disregard by parents. Also, little carelessness from the partner can be interpreted as a rejection because the feeling of rejection is already planted through other important relationships of our past.

We can't get to the origin of emotions if we reject what we feel in the start. If we deny our emotional state, it will not tell us anything about us. If we accept it, we have the opportunity to experience and revive discarded parts of ourselves. People who have "I-don't-exist feeling" does not accept themselves because they don't consider themselves worthy enough. Acceptance is a panacea for everything. Instead of looking for others to accept you, try to start providing it for yourself.

I understand that on paper all this seems easy. Accepting yourself is a difficult task for many, but not impossible. It is the only way to happiness and development. Every time you accept totally what you feel some sparkling doors are opening like in magic.

And, finally, acceptance of our feelings makes us honest to ourselves. We recognize that we are not perfect, we all have good and bad sides, and that we are all sometimes tired or cramped, but it's all a part of us that makes us special and very much like all the others. By accepting yourself, accepting others becomes a much easier task, and therefore life becomes more beautiful. Is not that a small price to pay for happiness?

My personal advices on how to accept yourself absolutely

Accepting yourself completely is equal to loving yourself completely as great writer Oscar Wilde said, "to love oneself is the beginning of a lifetime romance." Believe me, it is just the way Wilde said it. It took me many years first to realize that I do not accept myself, especially my introversion and it also took me many years to accept and love myself just the way I am.

How do you feel when you think that you are supposed to love yourself foremost? Do you find this idea repugnant, you might think that is selfish, or you think that this is impossible as I once thought? How many times have you heard "before you can love someone, you have to love yourself "? Although it is a cliché, many people feel uncomfortable when they hear something like this; some do not even understand what this is really about. From where does this discomfort come when you think about one and only person with whom you will certainly spend all your life and with whom you will share in detail all downs, ups, successes and all life dramas?

"The most terrifying and the most beautiful thing in the world are to accept someone completely". It is the sentence from already mentioned Karl Gustav Jung, one of the founders of analytical psychology. So, to love ourselves, we have to do exactly the scariest: to know and accept ourselves completely. Why is it sometimes so difficult?

Spin the wheel back and remember all those parental screaming, "How long are you going to make troubles and you're bearing attention to yourself ... You just want to be the center of attention, although you keep your mouth shut all the time." The tone of this sentences was always reproachful, angry, and usually that is what we get when we disturbed a life routine (in whose establishment, we did not participate), or when we try to step out, do some "unusual" step or implement one of our hidden ambition, desire, and talent. Even then, as we were children, we could create the idea that expressing our personality, what we carry in ourselves and accepting our desires actually brings nothing but trouble and criticism.

Even then was planted the seed of disliking ourselves and having the lack of positive image on ourselves that prevented us from self-love. I do not know about you, but it happened to me.

Numerous times I was reproached that I am clumsy, that I don't know how to talk to people or something like that. But now I realize that my extrovert mother wished all the best for me in life and thought she was teaching me to "fight and impress." I did not "fight or impress" in her way, but I can say I am more successful in life than 80 percent of my peers, of course under the success rate here I mean what is commonly called this way: good job, family, etc.

As we grow and develop, we may often feel unwanted, unloved, or afraid that our feelings and needs are not important or valuable. Many of us were raised by parents unable or insufficiently mature to show an unconditional love that belongs to child or to indicate acceptance and emotions. Instead of joy, approval, love, in the eyes of parents who have shaped the image of ourselves we've often seen anger, fear, sadness, apathy or lack of interest.

As we grow, we have to deal with the environment which is often very rash and labels people on this and that. So again we begin to question our attitudes, we want to fit in and not bulging, and this often means that we need to choke the most beautiful and best in ourselves that makes us unique individuals.

Mae West, American actress and sex symbol knew said "I do not love myself, I am crazy about myself!"

But when I talk about self-love, I do not advocate self-centered, exclusive, selfish or euphoric, irrational, narcissistic love which endangers the needs of others for the sake of our own. Focusing on yourself and loving yourself, you do not ignore the others. On the contrary, very often we able to provide more for those we care about if we care about ourselves. Maintaining a balance is necessary: you cannot give to others if you are not at the same time giving to yourself. It sounds cold, mathematical, but you must admit that it sounds like common sense. We have to "feed" ourselves first, so we can have something to share with others.

However, loving oneself is for many people experience that is hard to attain. People, especially introverted or thinking people, are often unaware that they are bad to themselves or that they do not to take into account their needs and desires and are not in touch with their true character. Such people are often not very kind to the voice that comes to them from their heart and reveals their true qualities. People who do not love themselves can spend a lifetime looking for peace, fulfillment and joy in all the wrong places.

Do you find it difficult to accept a compliment? Are you often disrespectful to your own success, talking about yourself through ridiculing jokes that sound bitter to the careful listener? You might think that this is all irrelevant, but carefully, you might have already, unwittingly, struggling with a lack of self-love. However, what is good is that one can learn how to love himself. Self-love is a skill you can practice, if you weren't lucky to be taught self-love by your closest family and the environment in which you grew up.

Learn the skill of self-love

To begin, start at the base: act like you already love yourself the most. Indulge yourself as much as circumstances permit you to. Think what would you do for someone like you, and then do it for yourself, no matter if it's preparing a delicious dinner, an exclusive weekend, buying a new wardrobe that you do not really need. Eat a healthy diet, exercise, show yourself to love your body and that you care for him.

After that, sail back in your past and remember the things you want to do while growing up, and have not had the opportunity, time, or space for it. Recall your talents that never develop and experiment with them. Maybe your parents thought you were gifted in mathematics, so today you're a successful manager who superbly handles with numbers. But inside there is still a dancer, painter or writer who invites you to unscrew the music and play, to take a little paintbrush, colors or start to write.

The fact that you have not used your talents does not mean that they disappeared. Maybe one of them will never give birth to a successful career, but it will become part of your personality which will enrich your everyday life or will reveal new dimensions of yourself and thus change your perception of the environment.

To love ourselves, we need to build self-esteem, and it can be reached by obtaining approval and support for what we do, and we think we want. Again, many grow up without a real recognition in an environment in which the error scolds while successes are taken for granted. Come out of that model of behavior and begin to be your own greatest support.

Surely you are surrounded by wonderful friends and colleagues, people you respect and love, with whom you share their problems and yours and for whom you always have time for comforting sentences, walking, infinitely understanding and assuring them that they are strong and that they are not wrong. And how much time, energy and understanding, as well as fine words, you have for yourself? When did you last talk with yourself about the things you are going through, commended yourself for many successes that you accomplish and tell to yourself that you are special, strong and perfect just the way you are?

Probably the most of you are a better support to others than you are for yourself. Moreover, you are likely sharper to yourself, more stringent and more demanding than what would have been to anyone else. Okay, on the way of personal affirmation and character building, we must be disciplined, but there must be limits. Maybe you have set your limits a little too far because you simply have not learned to love yourself?

Maybe it's time to make your inner dialogues become gentler, more considerate and start talking with yourself as you talk to your partner, friend, cousin to whom you want to help to overcome the bad period. From time to time is not bad to replace self-criticism with the positive, encouraging thoughts for your good mood and, long term, it is valuable for your self-esteem. Sustain your ego from time to time, let him grow and feel strong and powerful.

If we love ourselves, we need to encourage ourselves to re-explore, to experiment, to show our feelings, express opinions and develop our individuality. We need to learn that the only person who can tell us that something we are doing is wrong or not is the one we see in the mirror every day.

When you love yourself, you will learn to trust your feelings. It will not be necessary for someone else to tell you what to wear and what to think since you will no longer seek refuge in other people. When we really love ourselves, we will not go into the relationships that we are aware are the compromises or we choosing it because it is unbearable to be alone, or we simply needed to take care of someone.

Are you afraid that you will not meet expectations in a love relationship, you will not "get" love and you'll be left behind? The good news for you is that love is not something you should deserve. Show your partner that you care about him, but also show him that you respect yourself, your time and your needs. So, he will fall in love with you a bit more.

Make a decision today that you will love yourself unconditionally because love should be like that: unconditional. Start to love all that you are, that you have done and everything you think and feel. Love your spirit and love your body just the way it is. When you succeed in that, when you get to know yourself and then learn to love your uniqueness, you will give yourself the most precious gift in the world that lasts a lifetime.

1.4. Tips for speaking in public

Speaking in public is a problem for almost all of us, but for introvert person it can be a nightmare. There are some advices you can apply if you have to speak in public that will ease your performance and save you from filling guilty or a shame, which are, as I already said, futile and destructive feelings. Imagine that even Mark Twain thought that speaking in public can be a real trouble by saying "The human brain is a funny thing. It starts to work at the time of birth and turns off when we got up to speak in public".

1. Prepare yourself well

Let me tell you just a bit about me and public speaking. I work as a teacher in elementary school for over ten years now, but when I first started it was a living hell for a person like me. Before each and every class, my heart was pounding and my head was spinning with fear. What was most helpful for me then, and it helps me a lot even now is detailed preparation with the time frame. So, make a detailed preparation of exposure if you supposed to speak in front of smaller or larger group of people. If you make preparation, you will be much safer and it will affect your entire appearance in public. The voice and the presentation will look safer and more relaxed.

Do not allow yourself not to understand the subject enough. You should believe in what you're saying. When we are well versed in the content and have sufficient knowledge of what we present, there is a reduction of uncertainty, and, therefore, a reduction in the fear of public appearance.

Of course, I do not think that you should write for hours your preparation with each word that comes to your mind. Sit down and write how you have decided your exposure should look like. Highlight the main points of the speech and next to each write a description of what you want to talk about in chronological order. Preparation reduced my fear of public exposure for more than 50% and made me feel safer which greatly improved my performance.

2. Public speaking is acting

I was reading some article where is discussed whether public speaking is acting or not. I must tell you from my experience that in some way it is. It is just the nature of speaking in front of group of people. It is not the same as when you are speaking with your friend or a close relative. You are out "on the stage" and you are performing in some way.

That shouldn't bother you a lot, it can actually help you investigate and show off your other psychological traits. For example, you may come to the conclusion how mentally strong you are as I did. You can even act for real and make your public speaking more engaging for you and your listeners. Maybe you can't see it now, but public speaking can be a real joyride.

3. Breathing

I suppose this isn't something new for you to hear that a proper use of your breathe can make you be more relaxed and thus more focused. Actually, when we are upset by something, we lose our focus which makes us mentally disturbed and dysfunctional. So proper breathing is one of the most important fittings you can make just before your public speech. Let me show you how I do it and it never let me down. After this quick breathing meditation, I can talk in public with no jitters at all.

First, you have to decide that you want to focus on your breathing and let go of everything else. Inhale through your nose and exhale through your mouth. When breathing in slowly and deeply inhale the air (counting 4 seconds for the entire breath). It is important that the air first fills the lower part of the lungs (with eject out the abdomen), and then the middle and at the end the upper part of the lungs. You should keep the air for some time (4-

5 seconds) and then slowly (in the thawing of at least 5 seconds) slowly exhale.

It is recommended that when you exhale, you imagine that you discharge from all the tension, nervousness and fear. After this first round, you should take a little break and then repeat the procedure several times more. Five times is enough for you to feel like a reborn. You do not have to look for a secluded place for this quick meditation; no one will even notice you are relaxing. You do not even need to close your eyes, but if it helps you to concentrate close them.

4. Visualization

Many people are mostly visual types and some scientific studies show that visualization can be a good preparation for almost anything. Whether we are learning how to act while visualizing or it's just that nice pictures in our mind are making us happy, isn't that important. What is important is that visualization really works. 5 to 10 minutes a day of visualizing, before you need to go speaking public, are enough.

Although we cannot precisely determine when humans first began to consciously use visualization to create results, it is known that the scientist Nikola Tesla used the power of creative visualization to create ingenious inventions that significantly improved the mankind. I read that during the seventies of the last century, the Russians began to apply creative visualization to achieve better results in sports. They found that on the occasion of visualization, although totally still, athletes activate the same muscle groups that are otherwise active in the training. They conducted a test where there were two test groups. The first group trained with the load while the other group just visualized exercises. Think about it. After three months, the first group increased its muscle mass by 30%, while the second group increased their muscle mass by 13.5% only with visualization!

Try a visualization technique which has become an integral part of the training of a growing number of professional athletes. It is proven to enhance physical and psychological reactions. The more vivid is your experience of confidence and relaxation; it will be easier to remember those feelings when you need them. When practicing, imagine the scene with as much details. Point out the details on which you respond well. If you can, visualize with as much colors and details. This exercise changes the attitude to the troubled situation. This kind of visualization with the feeling of good emotions arising from the pretty pictures highly relaxes and increases self-confidence.

5. The audience is not your enemies

Do not think of an audience as enemies because they are not. Nobody wants to see you embarrassed in some way unless they are psychopaths. Have you ever seen someone publicly disgraced and what did you feel at that moment? Shame, of course, because one member of human species is disgraced. The same way others feel since they are also humans. Experts suggest different methods which reduce the subjective experience of the importance of the people sitting in the audience. Some suggest that you should imagine people in comic release, or even naked, however, I believe that this exaggeration is not necessary and can even turn your focus from the essential things.

6. Affirmations

Someone spunk himself with the sentence "I will blow them all," someone says, "It will be good," someone is trying to remain completely calm. Effective methods used in REBT psychotherapy, which reduce anxiety and build confidence is STOP technique and the use of affirmative sentences. Negative thoughts like "Jitters will eat me" should be first stopped by the rational mind: "STOP! These thoughts are not good for me. "Then, you should be encouraged by two to three affirmative sentences that will help you to restore confidence. E.g. "I was struggling a lot in order to prepare this and now I choose this performance to be excellent. Even though I get confused, nothing terrible will happen to me. "

7. If you, however, "suddenly block"

Regardless of all the preparation and all the tricks it can always happen that in the middle of a presentation or speech you just stop! What then? You start to panic. There are a few things that you can always do and continue where you left off. If you stop, you can repeat briefly what you were talking about or to show some material that you have prepared. You can, also, just admit that you're a human being of flesh and blood and that you have stage fright!

This last will definitely be well received because most people have already experienced it. What blocks you is the fear of stage and fear of public appearances! But always keep in mind that you are invited one to speak because you have a lot to say and share with the audience.

A few more tips for overcoming stage fright that helps me

- Memorize the first few sentences, this will help you not to confuse.

- Do not start speaking until the audience is quite.

- Start your speech with a smile on your face as this is the signal that you are sure of what you say.

- Speak slowly enough.

- Take breaks; they are good for you and the audience. Give you the opportunity to think about the next sentence, and the audience to think about what you're saying.

What's the worst that can happen to you? Fainting?

I never heard nor seen anyone fainted from stage fright. When I ask people what they anticipate as the worst thing that can happen while speaking in front of the public, they mostly say, "To stop and that I cannot continue - to block." However, although almost all are afraid of this, even the blockade is not something that happens often, especially not if someone is well prepared.

So, the terrible things you think might happen most often does not happen, but it is very harmful to think that way. By reiterating that something bad can happen, we actually increase the possibility for error. Hence, what we have "predicted" can actually happen, no matter how unlikely it is. You should consider this as a psychological rule and pay more attention to what you think.

Practice

The time has come to try all that you have heard and read. Prepare now and try to simulate. I would not recommend an overuse of exercise on a daily basis because your voice will echo in your head, and it can be very burdensome. The practice thus includes simulating the entire situation. The audience may be your friends or family, and if not, you can set various items in front of you. As children are very imaginative, they use dolls this way to play. So, can you if you do not like bothering close people although they can advise you and items can't.

1.5. Tips for online communication

We are all familiar with the fact that online communication in the modern world is more than essential. Communicating via social networks and emails became the leading form of communication, both in business and in personal relationships. It is very important to be open and ready for online communication. Some people say that an introvert rule in online communication, but is that true for all the introverts? I do not think so. Introverted people are studious, and, therefore, slower, as well as insecure while communicating with strangers, so they can also have difficulties in online communication. There are some actions and tips that can make them communicate effectively online. But it needs to be applied, not just read. Essentially, practice is mother of all skills and that counts for everything.

1. Should I put my picture or not?

A team of Finnish psychologists came to the conclusion by research that introverted people less put their photos on their social profiles and it would be better they do. In fact, people have more confidence in those who have their picture on their social profile. I suppose you prefer to see how someone, with whom you want to communicate, looks and not to admire a beautiful landscape or a quote. How true this is, I can confirm from personal experience because I never accept to communicate with someone who does not have a personal picture on their profile. I always wonder what does he/she hides, and it is boring also. So, set your picture so that people would know with whom they communicate.

Finnish psychologists also claim that it is much easier to fake extroversion, but introversion. But do you really want to introduce yourself as someone different than you really are? The best would be to put a nice photo that reflects your character, although it would not hurt if you smile. Just do not put a picture from your identity card; we all look horrible on them by some weird default.

2. Take your time

Before, I did not indulge in online discussions and conversations because I felt that I needed a lot of time to write a post that I like and that the speed of response in the online communication is at price, which represented a lot of stress for me. E.g. I do not like grammatically incorrect sentences to see on the internet nor in the internal communication through social networks. At one point, I thought that literacy isn't that important and that I would communicate more quickly if do not think much about it. However, I realized that I'm wrong and that me spending the time to write a grammatically correct sentence brings me the benefits not harm. So I decided to give myself time if I want to do things right.

In this busy world we live in, it is particularly difficult for introverts to manage because the general perception is that everything has to be fast and that time is money. However, good things take time, especially the depth of thinking in which introverts are better than introverts. So, take your time to think if you needed, do not post or message nonsenses just to keep the conversation going.

You may think "Okay, but if it's something is related to business or career, I have to be fast." Well, you do not have to be that fast, it is pretty much the same in this area. You can write your correspondent that you need some time to think or that you have to investigate on something. You can also say you'll be back in a second or ask another question if you find some incomprehensible. People will honor your attention to details in business which is very rare these days. Remember: Good things take time and that is why the introverts are perfect for to create them.

3. I do not know people who will see my posts

This point follows the previous. If you said what you thought and spend some time writing it in a proper manner, don't you think you gave your best? Sometimes, you will get a positive feedback and sometimes negative, so what? I must notice that by doing this way while communicating online, I did not ever get a negative feedback and that is true. Maybe some people were not interested in what I got to say, but no one actually called me a moron, if you know what I mean.

In this way, most of the people I meet online thought my comments were on place and some were even posting me questions. You have to take your time and be yourself and the positive feedback will come for sure. That is why I said at the beginning that accepting yourself will bring you space to learn, improve and succeed.

1.6. Face to face communication

I suppose this type of communication is where most of the introvert persons feel some sort of difficulties since it is still an issue for me too, but not in the extent it was before when I was younger. The repetitive questions of others like "Why are you so silent?" or "Why are you so closed?" used to make me angry when I was a teenager and a bit older. I thought all those angry thoughts like "Why do you care?", "Because you are stupid and talking nonsenses" and alike.

What I have learned after, told me those angry self-talk came from my deep belief that I am not good enough, stupid and weird in some way. But, the truth is different. People are asking those from various reasons and none of them means they want to hurt your feeling or something. I came to the conclusion that followed reasons are the causes of those questions that irritate the introverts:

1. Someone likes you and wants to know you better.

2. People are generally afraid of something they do not know so they want to make themselves more comfortable in your society.

3. People want to help you in a way to be more open and there is nothing wrong with that.

1. Smile

Okay, if someone told me to smile in front of the people I am not that familiar too when I was a teenager, I would be very annoyed. I would say "I am not a cheat and I do not want to put on a fake smile. What is the point?" Well, now I know better. In a part about public speaking, I said the audience is not your enemy and the same goes for new people you meet. Nobody is saying that you need to be intrusive, but a slight smile, while meeting and listening to other people, will bring many benefits to you in communicating with others.

A smile in the first place means acceptance, and all people want to be accepted, no matter if some of them seem like they are full of self-confidence. A smile is also a sign that you are friendly so it will make people feel more relaxed in your company. Even a small curve line, something like a half-smile will be enough. Anything is better than inquiring, sulky look when you meet someone new or are in the company of people who you know less.

2. Eye contact is very important

Second important thing while talking with people is to look them in the eyes. You do not have to stare at someone since it is stupid and intrusive, but please look them in the eyes if you are speaking with them. We all know that eyes are perceived as windows of the soul, so why hiding your soul unless there is something to be hidden. I personally do not like people that are not looking in my eyes while speaking with me and I don't have time to research whether they are shy, hiding their attentions or just superficial.

When you are looking in someone's eyes while speaking with him, he feels important so he wants to tell the truth and show himself in the best light. But better than that is the fact that eye contact is somewhat more important than the words itself. Eye contact makes communication constructive and more honest. Regarding what I said about smile goes for eye contact too, and more: by looking people in the eyes you will know who to trust and who probably is not worth it. Keep in mind for your sake that people distinguish those who avoid eye contact mainly like someone who has something to hide.

3. First impression on business meetings

You will never have a second chance to make a first impression, and it follows that we are all aware of how it is crucial, especially in a professional world where first impressions dictate the tone of the conversation, interview or business relationship. We all realize that we need to do everything in our power to leave a positive first impression at the first business meeting. I will name two things below that I consider especially important for business and it goes together with a smile and a proper eye contact.

Some research shows that we only need a few seconds to get a first impression of the person we first see. An integral part of man's nature is that his first impression of someone is primarily formed on the basis of appearance, body postures, movements and behavior. It is important to note that first opinion can later be very difficult to change, especially if it's bad. Even if a person has a lot of other qualities, almost always we will again remember the bad first impression.

Therefore, regardless of whether you are beginning a career or you are already employed, it is desirable to adhere to business etiquette. In this way, there are great chances that your employer or business associates will acquire a good first impression of you. Later, it will be much easier for you to confirm the good opinion with your knowledge, skills and diligence.

It should be noted that business etiquette in any case does not involve abnormal behavior, acting and speaking untruths. On the contrary, such behavior can make you a problem because your true nature will be revealed once.

1. Align your back

Slouch is a sign of laziness, weakness or limp. In any case, it does not bind to any of the positive characteristics. The same goes for posture. So shoulders back and head up. Even if the person you communicate with does not pay attention to your posture, his / her subconscious is doing it and creating a picture of you, you do not want. On a subconscious level, you will not look desirable enough for that new job or a business contract. It isn't that hard to straighten your back, is it? I mean, if you want the job.

2. Firm handshake

This section continues to a right posture. How many times have you offered someone only your fingers to grip? This is really annoying for most people. Firm handshake speaks of confidence and determination of a person. However, if you overdo with the grip strength is no longer self-confidence, but brutalization. So safe and not limp handshake is a good introduction to the interview, but I would say for personal relationships too. The handshake should be accompanied by eye contact and a bit of a smile, of course.

3. Respect the terms

To be late for a job interview or business meeting in the beginning means a bad impression. It is almost certain that if you're prone to delay, you act as an unreliable person who does not respect other people's time. It is not advisable to come too early, too. Your early arrival can disrupt the plans of the person you are visiting or you can act impatiently.

4. **Kindness is always appreciated**

The man who, despite some pressures looks cheerful and smiling and who while talking with people patiently and actively listens to them may be considered polite. Kindness does not mean just to smile, always have the same intonation, nodding even when you should not. Courtesy primarily means to understand the interlocutor. Also, kindness implies patience and a willingness to make additional efforts in the conversation.

It would be advisable to make an extra effort in an important meeting for the job because it will surely pay off. People need to understand their introversion, but not to hide behind labels of introversion. It cannot be an excuse for each unsuccessful communication, whether on a personal or professional level. The comforting fact is that introverted people are much better at being polite than extroverts, but only when they invest some effort into it and do not see kindness as impersonation.

See more good reason to be kind

Kindness stimulates the production of serotonin. This hormone helps wounds heal faster, you feel calm and most of all you feel happy. However, the best thing is that kindness not only works well for you. The Nice and kind gesture will brighten the day to you, to whom you helped, and everyone who witnessed this act. The Nice and kind gesture will beautify a day, and you it will slow down your aging.

In addition, kindness accelerates the production of endorphins, a natural painkiller. When you are going and friendly toward people in your neighborhood, then your body produces oxytocin, also known as the hormone of embrace. This hormone strengthens social bonds, has a calming effect on the body, forcing you to be generous and to have more faith in people. In addition, oxytocin, which your body produces after a friendly gesture has a good influence on your immune system, but also to sexual maturity.

There is also evidence that compassionate people and those who are always ready to help others, have in their body two times more DHEA hormones, which slows down aging. Also, they have a 23 percent lower level of the hormone cortisol or stress hormones. So, even science has confirmed that the kindness is a good thing. So put a smile on your face for a start. I think these reasons are more than enough for you to practice kindness although you are "lost in your world".

Chapter 2:
How to be more courageous

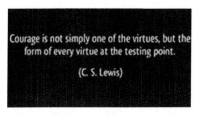

Courage is not simply one of the virtues, but the form of every virtue at the testing point.

(C. S. Lewis)

People often tend to underestimate introverted people, but they almost always pleasantly surprise those who listen to them carefully. Research shows that introverted people are much more specific in describing things; a simple and clear description leaves a much better impression on listeners. Compared with extroverts who tend to only scratch the surface, studies have shown that introverts go far more to the essence of things. In an introverted person, parts of the brain associated with vigilance, caution and motor skills are more developed. Simply put, introverted talk a little and think a lot. The problem occurs when they need to present their views and thoughts. Hence a simple question of how to develop determination, or more simply put courage necessary for success in all areas of life.

2.1. Courage is one of the qualities you can strengthen and develop

1. Do you want to dance?

I'll tell you a short story about me and a dance floor. Until I was 30, I have never danced in front of other people; it was something I thought I will never ever do in my life. I didn't dance neither at parties nor on my prom night. I didn't even dance on my wedding. Can you imagine that kind of blockage? I was terrified that someone may ask me for a dance so I always wore that "I'm not really interested" face. For your understanding, I love to dance and that is why I felt so miserable watching others dance in public like it was nothing.

One day I was at my friend wedding and they were all dancing not even trying to call me on a dance floor as they knew "I am not interested". At one point, something just snapped in me and I was thinking "I am 30; I will never be younger or more beautiful as I am now. My life is passing by and I am just sitting here captured by stupid thought in my head".

So, I got up and I danced more than three hours and I could dance the whole night, but the party was over. I was so happy and so were the people around me. We were all happy dancing and no one laugh at me. On the contrary, some of my friends told me I am a good dancer. Can you imagine that? I have spent 15 or more years waiting in my shell and in one moment, the shell was broken and I was so thrilled. Okay, I do not think you will learn from this story of mine how to be more courageous, but I hope you'll see what you are missing and maybe it will stimulate you to take actions.

2. Face your fears and doubts

If you want to overcome your fear, you will just have to face it. You can do something you haven't done before, simply to develop courage. For example, go rafting or climb a rock. I am joking a bit, but the essence stays. It does not matter what you have decided to do to develop courage, as long as it prompts you to deal with some sort of discomfort. Sorry, but every school pays. If you do not wish to make changes for the better, you won't and no one can make you do it. At the end, it is all about your own life journey and the feelings you have.

There is one interesting thing about not leaving your comfort zone. Ironically, taking risks and stepping out of the comfort zone and staying in the comfort zone are causing the same amount of fear. The only difference is that those who do not take the risk are taking care of important matters. Anyway, you will have to go through the fear and doubt, so it is better that it has some meaning and purpose.

3. Make a first step

You are for sure familiar of that popular phrase that a path of thousand miles begins with one step. This clause applies in general to all in life, but also for developing courage. The point is to make a step forward no matter how uncomfortable it may be for you. You have to endure if you want to progress and be satisfied with your life. Here, what, for example, can be the "famous" first step for you:

1. <u>Perform a conversation that you have been delaying for a long time</u>

   Most people avoid unpleasant and open discussions with employees, business partners or family members. For the introvert, it is a particular problem because they have a manner of hiding behind a mask of indifference or laziness. You do not have to insult anyone; just speak honestly about what lies at the heart. Respect the person you are talking to even though that person may play dumb or it is just one of those people who are difficult to talk with. Use your arguments and do not give up on them. This is the only way you can finish the conversation with dignity and without a sense of frustration.

2. <u>Do something you think you are clumsy at</u>

   Remember the story about the dance? Well, dance a bit although your cheeks may be red or your legs may be stiff. Swing a bit and then you will feel the music carries you. I must tell you that I truly appreciate those who dance although they are ashamed of it. I have a colleague, who dances at all gatherings and always has blushing cheeks while doing it. I really admire his courage.

Go out and play football or basketball. So what if you are not Lebron James or Messy? If that is something you want to do, but feel like you are clumsy, just do it. Conquer your fear by doing what you are afraid of. That is the only way, believe me. You got nothing just by reading the instructions, you have to apply it.

Maybe you are too shy and afraid to call someone for a date? Well, it really does not matter whether that person will reject you or not. The thing is that you are becoming courageous and that is what counts. It goes like this: the more you put yourself in situations that frighten you, the more courage you develop. Not much of a philosophy, but at the end all big things are very simple to know but sometimes hard to implement.

4. **Do you have the will to develop courage?**

Do not say "I do not know how to develop the will, first", as we are all aware that willpower comes with a need. The question is how strong your need is to have more courage and, therefore, do things you are dreaming of doing? Let's say, you are in a bad need for money since your frig is empty. What would you do? Lie back on your couch or do something about it?

I think this way: if you know there is someone who will help you with your need, there is a big chance you will not have the will to look for a new job opportunity those days or months. But, if there is absolutely no one to help you with your need, you would look for a job from dawn till sunrise and eventually after a couple of days you would find one. Excuse me if I'm wrong, but I just speak up from my own experience.

The best way to develop courage is to "throw yourself in the fire" as many times as possible. At one point, you will notice that it is not the fire at all and it was all an illusion of the mind who is anticipating reality based on previous anticipations that brought you discomfort. It is like a vicious circle that is interrupted as soon as you make the first step in a different direction.

Courage is not the absence of fear, but when we do something despite the fear. The absence of fear is trust. I think about having trust in life and feeling that there is a higher power that cares for us, and trust in yourself and feeling that this force in you.

Both the courage and the trust are virtues that we need to hone and cultivate. When I say virtues, it means that all of us have the seeds of trust and courage within ourselves, but we do not give them the opportunity to grow and proliferate. Well, in some people the virtues forever remain in seed form. And when I say hone and cultivate it means that we should disallow some pain and discomfort from stopping us, knowing that this is the only way ordinary stone becomes a diamond.

This means that in those situations that are most dreadful for us lay our greatest potential. And if we allow ourselves to go through the experience no matter how hard it is we allow the alchemy of life to happen.

Chapter 3:
How to boost your confidence

Confidence has always been a synonym for success, leadership or for the fulfillment in life. Our time is no exception, and today we have a lot of published books that deal with this topic. At the same time, the demand for the services of a psychologist, organizing seminars, lectures and pieces of training is increasing.

What is so good in confidence or what it is a confident person?

A confident person uses offered chances and believes that his abilities are sufficient to perform every task before him. Confident people always talk openly about their feelings, wishes, and requirements. They are always able to establish contact, to start and end the conversation. These people are not afraid to set new goals and enthusiastically take action for their implementation.

The truth is that each of us is good at something and not so good at something else. So nobody is a super-perfect hero who never doubts himself and achieves everything he wants. The truth is that all of us sometimes feel insecure and like a failure. But there are certain traits typical for confident people:

- They are secure in themselves and believe that they are capable even they fail or make mistakes

- They think about what really matters to them and follow their interests and goals (instead of waiting for somebody to "push" them in a right direction)

- They believe that they can influence what happens to them, and are determined and persistent in dealing with problems

- They are less influenced by others and are more willing to advocate for their own attitudes

- They take better care for themselves because they like themselves and are important to themselves, and because they believe that they can influence things and achieve the desired outcomes

- They are more successful in the implementation and development of new skills

- Problems and failures are seen as a learning opportunity, not an insurmountable obstacle and a sign that they are "total failures"

- They express themselves better in relationships and more clearly define their lifestyle (they know what they like to listen, communicate openly and stand up for what they believe). Confident people do not allow others to treat them badly and take care for themselves (or seek help if they cannot protect themselves).

Those who are unsure do not have sufficient confidence in relationships with other people and are afraid of judgments so they rarely express their opinion. Insecure people cease to be active, not only in achieving their goals but, in general. They are losing faith in themselves fast and believe that their goals are unrealistic.

People without much self- confidence in solving problems and making decisions rely more on others than on themselves and are afraid to expose and show initiative for fear of criticism.

- They do not appreciate their accomplishments and have a negative judgment of their own appearance and behavior

- Unfortunately, these people are often the victims of abuse and violence because they feel helpless and believe they can't do anything to protect themselves from the abuse (this is not true, if something like this happens, be sure to ask for help! No one has the right to insult, call derogatory names, and mock or ignore your needs and desires in a rough way.).

Thinking bad about yourself or being ashamed of yourself makes you feel unhappy and prevent you from expecting nice things in the future.

How to estimate the level of self-confidence?

Each of us feels tense in unfamiliar situations and that's perfectly normal. If the anxiety and numbness follow you all your life, even in the most ordinary situations, you should change your attitude. It is not good to "tuck our tail" and "lick our wounds" in some hidden place, avoiding people, because that way we will just learn to turn our head away from problems, and life will take place somewhere far away from us. As I have already said, action cures the fear so it would be best that we deal with troubles and try to beat them.

Here are some simple tips on how to deal with fears and increase confidence:

1. Imitate self-confident people

Pay attention to the person who has the confidence and try to copy her style of communication. Imitate her voice, attitude, appearance and it will not take much time for you to develop the true confidence within yourself. I heard that this way of developing social skills really helped many introverted and shy persons to begin to live life as they want, although this way of learning never came to my mind.

2. Do not nurture self-pity

If you are prone to self-criticism, try to replace negative thoughts with positive. If the inner voice is telling you that " you will fail, because you're a born loser ", then remind yourself that the most successful people have learned from their mistakes. With this attitude, you will most certainly use the next opportunity in the right way. After all, once you truly realize how beautiful life moments you're missing by wasting energy on self-pity, you will automatically stop doing that to yourself.

The feeling of self-pity is one of the roots of many problems and failures and occurs as a result of some event that you experience. The self-pity is developed in childhood and its role is to reduce the pain of unpleasant situations. People copy this feeling from the older ones (parents, environment) and it should disappear as you grow older. However, this is often not the case, but self-pity remains in your life, and can become a habit that is hard to eradicate.

Self-pity can cause many negative emotions and as such has immensely destructive effects on your life. People often use the problems in their life in order to induce a feeling of self-pity. They do not realize that they often evoke problems themselves (or they turn a harmless situation into a problem), just to feel self-pity and play the victim. At the same time, the feelings of 'righteous' anger only complement the whole picture.

When in your life there is self-pity, you can hardly live a life filled with love, gratitude and gifts sent to you by the universe. However, if you understand this and try to eradicate the habit of self-pity, your life will be filled with love, happiness, and success. Feel free to ask the universe to help you do that!

3. Expand your comfort zone

It is known that people feel most comfortable in a family environment, with loved ones, or if they practice some known activity. Psychologists call this phenomenon the comfort zone. By expanding the circle of friends, learning new skills, even only in order to overcome psychological barriers, you are expanding the limits of your comfort zone and become more confident in your abilities. Expanding the comfort zone is often difficult for introverted people because they are in large numbers inert. However, when an introvert decides to get out of his comfort zone, he really makes fundamental changes in his behavior and point of view.

You can start by doing small things you have never done before just to see some other perspectives. It will be fun if nothing else.

Live in the present

To live every moment of your existence is real life. There is no room for fear, anxiety or discomfort, and there are many reasons not to live in the distant past. Do not let yourself become a worn out " archival record ', and to constantly scroll the same things from the past. Again, it is not even good to live in an uncertain future. You should try to live and enjoy right here and right now. The whole New Age teaching is based on this and I support it and I do everything I can to live in the here and now.

There are different techniques that can help you be more in the present moment like meditation, yoga and reading spiritual books. I highly recommend you that you do that, no matter if you are an introvert, extrovert or something in between.

Insist on your "space"

Do not be afraid that you will be branded as selfish, if you store your things, your peace, and freedom. If you allow everyone to take things from you or endangers your peace, it's just the reverse side of self-doubt.

Express your feelings openly

Express your emotions freely both positive and negative, without fear that someone will not like it. This is really important for introverted people because they often think that expressing feelings verbally is not so important, so most often they lose friends and partners because of this lack in communication.

To be able to express feelings of happiness or even sadness is incredibly healthy. Scientists have long believed that what we feel has a significant impact on how our body reacts. When we are happy, our body feels cared for. When we are sad or angry, our body also needs to throw a little tension. Expressing feelings and emotions is important because it serves as an exhaust valve. Why is it dangerous to have any negative feelings within yourself? When you think about it, all those repressed negativity has "to go" somewhere. In the most unfortunate cases, this negative energy manifests itself as a disease. I can't highlight enough how important is for introverts to express their feelings as it is important for those who are close to them.

Accept your imperfections

No one is perfect. I have already devoted a good part of the book to this topic. You should calmly think about your mistakes and failures because only those who do nothing doesn't make mistakes.

The human being isn't perfect, and a great number of people carry some part of themselves which they consider dissatisfying. This dissatisfaction may be work-related, stress and frustration that is experienced in the workplace or lack of employment. Also, we can be dissatisfied with handling our relationship with parents, problematic love or friendly relations that are under some tension, and the like. Each of us will in a different way process the situations described above. But to get to grip on them, we have to admit ourselves certain facts. No matter how discouraging that, conditionally said, "negative part" of our personality is, the first step in understanding ourselves, and that parts of the personality that we recognize as our imperfections.

What we call imperfection in us has to be analyzed objectively and compassionate from a position of objective observer who knows that, no matter how much we are discontent, it can gradually be transformed. Otherwise, there is a pain, fear, and other negative emotions. When we collect the courage to look at ourselves, it is necessary to ask someone who knows us well to tell us their opinion about us. Because, even if it is one person, we know that we can be with her without a mask, and that in itself is already a healing.

Pay attention to your strengths rather than your weaknesses

Insecure people are much more oriented to their failures and shortcomings but on their strength and success. Write a list of your 10 positive traits, powers or successes and read it every day (or at least when you "fall into a crisis"). At the end of the day pay attention to the successful and good situations and things that happened to you in the day. Discover how you contributed to it ("my friend helped me - and I contributed to building this friendship!"). Be proud of your accomplishments. What are your strengths? If listing your good sides is a problem to you, you can ask a dear friend or family member who loves you to point you what they appreciate in you.

Be realistic about your weaknesses and mistakes.

Learn from the mistakes of yours. See what you can do and what skills you need to develop and work on them. Everyone has their less developed points; it is not a sign that we are inadequate. We just got the parts of ourselves on which we can work with the effort to improve it. The guilt and self-pity wasn't good for anyone.

The experience of success motivates us and raises our confidence.

Recognize the success you have achieved! Maybe you're so hard on yourself if and when you succeed you do not prescribe it to your skills than to fortunate circumstances or others. Set realistic criteria for success because if these criteria are too high you will experience just a bit of success, so you will never be satisfied. Always remember your successes that you are proud of.

Change the focus!

Instead of worrying, "if I fail", try to avoid mistakes focusing on achieving objectives and developing the requisite skills and knowledge. Credit yourself for hard work and effort and not only for the achieved results.

Your present reality that makes all that you feel today, and you think of yourself is the result of your emotional focus. If you do not like your present reality, it is not a big deal, you can change it.

To make the desired change occur, it is necessary for you to first release existing unpleasant feelings about everything that you want to change. This step is absolutely necessary because it is physically impossible to accept and apply new knowledge until you are pulsing current unpleasant feelings because they are your physical proof that you have a problem. When there is no physical evidence, there is no problem!

The truth that has long been known is following: No one can feel at the same time good and bad feelings. It is possible to rapidly move the focus from any feeling to another, but it is physically impossible to focus on both the feelings at the same time. In accordance with the law of nature, you always get the results that are fully in accordance with your choice of your emotional focus.

Persevere in dealing with obstacles

Obstacles and temporary failures are parts of the path to success. Faults are not the test of our own powers. If you currently do not know how to deal with something, it does not mean that you will never solve these problems. Do not lose hope, rather examine the situation and see what you can do differently. The obstacles can strengthen us and "force" us to draw additional power, develop new skills or find support and advice.

I truly believe that those who are successful are those who stayed on their path regardless of the obstacles they were faced with.

Stop comparing with others

Instead, compare with yourself. For example, how much did you make today compared to yesterday or a month or a year ago? Commend yourself for progress and set further goals.

Most often we compare ourselves with people we know, once we envy them, and sometimes we are happy that we are better, but this is a big mistake because often we cannot realistically see them. When we compare with people whose opinion we respect the fact is we are facing the best version of that person and the worst version of you. This triggers negative feelings such as jealousy, which is very destructive to the psyche especially if it lasts for a long time. The excessive comparison may lead to depression and anxiety.

However, there is a constructive way to do so, in situations when someone's success motivates us to develop and improve our skills. Also, if you cannot resist this habit from childhood, compare yourself from different life periods, analyze where you were and what you were doing five or ten years ago, how did you look, what you enjoyed, with whom you have socialized and how did you spend your free time.

Take a good care for yourself

Listen to your needs and feelings. If you are sad, seek solace. If you need support, ask for it. If you're angry because you do not like the way someone treats you, you have the right to show it. If you want time for yourself, or something does not suit you, you have a right to say it. Discover which situations worry you, why and act to change what you do not like.

You should also take a good care of your body although I know that introverts doesn't care too much about it, but I truly hope you will not be sorry one day.

Stop worrying what others think about you

It is natural that we want to be loved by others and to make a good impression. However, exaggerated worry about it means to be sensitive to some passing comments and disappointments. While you care what other people think about you, they probably care what you think about them. Therefore, say to yourself, "Okay, I'd like others to like me, but it is not possible to please everyone. It's okay if someone thinks that I am not absolutely cool. I have important people (friends, family ...) that appreciate me. The most important thing is that I know I'm okay. "

Examine your success criteria

How good and successful you have to be to start appreciating yourself and be proud of yourself? Is only the best good enough for you? Do you measure with the same strict criteria all the others? Are you alleviating your successes or interpret them as good circumstances?

3.1 Develop the skills necessary for success.

Today we know that to succeed in life it is important to know and to stand up for yourself, communicate clearly, solve problems and deal with stress. Life is a life-long development of skills and learning.

Strong and cheerful

Instead of "How stupid and poor I am" or "I was being silly," say to yourself, "Okay, I'm not happy that I didn't pass this test, I got a bad grade. I have to plan how to correct it. I can do it, it's not so bad. It will be hard, but I've dealt with difficult situations before. I can seek help ". Think about what would be your advice to a dear friend in a similar situation if you wish to encourage and support him. Be as good to yourself as you are to others. Do not continuously spin the movie with old failures and situations when you felt ashamed.

Remember that some of this situation will be a source of laughter one day. Ask yourself, "will this situation will be very important to me in 10 years?" Why to wait for 10 years, change the point of view now and rather direct your thoughts on the present time and future steps.

Set life goals

Life is a process of achieving the goals. So, set your goals, short and long term, and their implementation will help you to achieve a much higher degree of confidence. Of course, you will not be able to do any of these things if you are lazy.

Use affirmations daily (they work on me)

Affirmations are essentially auto-suggestions or statements that we say to ourselves. They can be positive or negative and, depending on how often we use them, strongly affect our lives. By using positive affirmations, we can achieve better results in all aspects of life. We can form a better image of ourselves, raise self-esteem, achieve goals faster, gain or change habits, heal and more. We can also rinse our brains if we use negative affirmations such as "I do not deserve this and that", "I'm not good enough" and the like.

How do the affirmations work?

By repeating the affirmations for some time, we can form new mental concepts in our subconscious or change an existing one. These mental concepts in our subconscious will then affect our thinking, our behavior, and our actions. They form our reality. In essence, affirmations are only one part of the positivity and happiness to which we aspire.

Write them down

It is best that you write your affirmations. When we do not feel the best is much easier to read the affirmation than to seek it in the chaos of thoughts. Maybe you think this is stupid, but that's just the way I thought before I decided to give it a try and it really works but you need to be persistent.

Think about your needs

Formulate affirmations according to your needs. Since we are all unique and have different goals, ideas and habits, there is no single affirmation for all of us. So think about your goals, habits you want to acquire or change, the events you want to experience, feelings that you want to be part of your reality, define affirmation for yourself and write them down.

Speak them in the present tense

Going through my examples you may have observed that they are all imposed at present. When are imposed in the present, powerful emotions that you feel raises a whole series of energy and thought processes and change your subconscious. Feel the difference between "my life would be perfect," and "my life is perfect." When you say "my life would be perfect", your subconscious store the event for an indefinite period of time, just as it is the case with the objectives.

The emotion is very important

Try to feel the powerful emotion when you say the affirmation, and the faster you will achieve results. Please note that for someone who has a lot of problems in life to feel the right emotion while using the affirmation "my life is perfect" is quite impossible because the idea of a perfect life and that person are not on the same wavelength. In this case, more effective affirmation would be "things are changing for the better," or "I feel the improvement in this or that aspect of life" because it would trigger stronger emotions.

How to use affirmations

Affirmations should be pronounced as often as possible. In most cases the habit is formed after 3 weeks, 21 days, and sometimes it takes more because our adopted concepts are too hard to break. Repeat your affirmations at least 30 days in order to feel their effect. If in the meantime emotions change, modify the affirmation and move on.

3.2 Meditate on daily basis

Meditation can help you a great deal if you are an introverted person to easily and quickly process information from the outside world, and be much more confident and calm. I speak all these things from my personal experience because after a hard day in school during which I met many people and children, my senses are overstimulated and I feel as if my whole body is trembling. Meditation helped me a lot and still helps me to clear my mind and balance my emotions and that is why I strongly recommended it to introverted people.

Breathing is the starting and finishing point of all types of meditation. We "carry" our breath anywhere we are at all times, so it's a refuge, it helps us to focus on the moment in which we find ourselves and not to be distracted with a million thoughts that spin in our head. I will give you the quick course in meditation I practice and which helped me a lot to be more productive and more satisfied with my life experience.

Meditation has become a true need in fast modern world. Many researches have been done on the impact of childhood stress on one's adulthood. If we were scared and inhibited child, we continue to act this way when we grow up. Introducing the practice of meditation in our life will help us to deal better with our thoughts and emotions and to learn how to pay more attention both on the inside and the outside world.

1. Sit in a comfortable position with your legs crossed and your back straight. You can also lie on your back, stretched out, with a firm pillow or rolled up towel under your knees. You should extend your arms at an angle of 45 degrees to the torso. Although Zen meditation is called sitting meditation, you need to adapt it to yourself. The same is true for your child, the only thing is that kids will more likely fall asleep if you tell them to lie down and meditate.

2. Inhale and exhale quietly through your nose. Feel each breath as it passes through your torso. Imagine your breath is going through the parts of your body. The point is to try to constantly re-focus on your breath no matter how diverse thoughts want to distract you from focusing on your breath.

3. Notice how your breath changes as you focus on it, and how you deal with these changes and your consciousness. In fact, a more concrete explanation is that the role of the "witness" will occur while you observe your breathing and it will make you more and more relaxed. Also, when you find that a "witness" in you observes your breathing and your thoughts, your higher consciousness awakens.

4. When your thoughts start to wander, slowly redirect your attention to breathing. This redirection should be as neutral as it can be, that is, without judging yourself and your thoughts. In meditation, the thoughts are not divided into good and bad, they are more experienced as casual passers-by. It is your decision whether you will follow a certain thought or not.

5. Start to run your breath to parts of your body that you feel "are not breathing". Imagine that your torso is a vessel and try to actively send the breath to places where you usually don't feel it, such as the pelvis or lower back. Do not do it by force, but rather allow the breath to follow your

conscience. In fact, this is the essence of being in the body or mindfulness.

6. At the end of the process, shake your fingers on hands and feet and stretch your arms and legs. If you are lying down, turn to the side and take a break before you return to a sitting position. Stand up slowly, lifting the torso first and then a head.

3.3 My 10 ways to immediately lift the self-confidence

Although many factors affect your self-confidence which you cannot control, there are those which you can consciously make to boost your self-confidence. By using the following strategies, you will be able to move mental boundaries and achieve your goal. Maybe this will sound like a cliché, but it has always helped me especially when I need to pass from one closed environment and to go among the people, because this kind of transition is always more or less stressful for me.

1. Put on a modern and beautiful clothes

Although the suit does not make the man, definitely affects how you feel about yourself because you are the one who is most aware of your public appearances. If you do not look good, it changes the way you represent yourself, and the way you communicate with other people. However, this does not mean you have to spend too much money on clothes. It is enough to have a few quality items instead of piles of cloth that after a few months can be discarded. Another tip, for which it took me years to adopt: buy a comfortable and beautiful clothing item, although is maybe more expensive instead of 10 things that will rot in your closet and you will never have anything to wear.

You may think of this as a cliché, but something had to be tried out or spoken by many to become a cliché, so I consider them to be thrust if you know what I mean.

2. Walk faster

One of the easiest ways to determine whether a person is secure and self-confident is to look at how he/she walks. People who are sure of themselves are walking quickly, because they go to a lot of places, meet many people and have some important tasks, you know what I mean? Even if you are not in a hurry, increase your self-confidence and accelerate the pace. If you are walking 25 percent faster, you will look and feel like you are very important. What can the art of acting make, you are not even aware of it until you try. You can try to walk quickly with the fixed back just to see the reactions of people around you.

3. Take a stand

Man's attitude says a lot about him. People with hunched shoulders and slow movements give the impression of people unsure of themselves. They are not satisfied with their lives and suffer from an inferiority complex. By exercising better attitude, your confidence grows. Stand up, raise your head and look people straight in the eye. So people will gain a positive impression on you, and you will feel more important.

The more you practice, the better you become like in everything in life.

4. Personal advertisements

One of the best ways to increase self-esteem is to listen to motivational speeches. Unfortunately, there is little chance of that. However, you can satisfy this need if you write a speech about yourself about 30 to 60 seconds long, where you can emphasize your goals and strengths. I recommend that you recite a speech in front of the mirror (or, if you prefer: to yourself) whenever you feel your confidence is falling.

5. Be grateful

When you too much focus on what you want, your mind tells you the reasons why you cannot have it and it points to retain your weaknesses. The best way to avoid this is a conscious concentration on being grateful. Every day, take the time to think about things that you should be grateful on. Remember the previous successes, unique skills and positive moments.

6. Compliment others

When you do not feel good about yourself, you can project this feeling on others in the form of gossip and rumor. To exit from this circle of negativity, make it a habit to praise others. Avoid conversations in which someone is gossiping, but discover a way to find only the good things in others because it is best for you to do.

7. Sit in the front rows

At school, at work, in public gatherings around the world, people often tend to sit in the back of the room. Many prefer the margins because they do not want or are afraid to be noticed. By deciding to sit in the first row, you can overcome the irrational fear and raise your confidence to a higher level, and also important people will notice you.

8. Speak more loudly

During group discussions, many people do not want to report to the word because they fear that others will think that what they say is stupid. This fear, however, is not justified because generally people are more accepting others than we think. Make sure you've at least once during the discussion took a word on the subject, you will become a better speaker, safe in your thoughts or maybe even recognized as a leader for your peers. I had this fear of speaking loud in the gatherings, but I beat it in the meetings of the teachers' council at the school where I work. The first time I applied to say something, my heart was pounding like crazy, and now that isn't a problem for me anymore.

9. Exercise

The appearance of your body says a lot about you. If you are out of shape, it is logical that you'll feel insecure, unattractive, and with less energy. If you practice, you will not only improve your physical appearance, but you will be more positive and energetic. I prefer some easy exercises.

10. Focus on contribution

People pay too much attention on themselves, ignoring the needs and desires of others. If at least for a second, you can stop to think only about yourself and pay attention to your contribution to society, you will not worry so much about your flaws. This way you will raise your self-esteem, be more efficient in everything you do and be recognized and rewarded for your success.

And now, as you read these tips, wear something nice, go out with friends, show your best side to the world and enjoy.

Chapter 4:
The good sides of being an introvert

I wrote this chapter not to make you happy about your good side or to make you sad about your bad side. I just want to point you how you can develop and improve.

4.1 Signs that reveal whether you are introverted

While the stereotypical point of view is that introverts are very easy to recognize, for example, they are those who at the parties will always stand by and fiddle with their phone. However, someone who interacts well in a group can also be an introvert. People often do not realize that they are introverts because they think introversion is about being shy but there are many signs that would indicate whether we are introverts. Check out some of them.

1. You struggle with small talk

I already said something about this subject, but I think introverted people should give a small talk a chance. It just means you should give people a chance by talking with them if they feel the need to tell you something.

2. You are going to parties, but not to meet people

If you are introverted, sometimes you may want to go to a social event but never do, or you go but do not meet new people. Most introverts at parties spend time with people they already know. If you happen to meet a new person, that's fine, but that was never your intention.

3. You often feel lonely in a crowd

If you feel like an outsider at social gatherings even if there are people you know present, you're probably an introverted type. Okay, I must say I still feel lost when I am in a crowd, and I just do not like it.

4. Networking causes hives

What is normal for some people, which is networking in order to achieve better business contacts," you feel fake.

5. Sometimes people tell you that you're "too intense"

If you are prone to deep philosophical discussions and cultivate a love for literature and films that are an intellectual challenge, most likely you're an introvert. ☐

6. You can easily be distracted

While extroverts are bored when they are not surrounded by enough variety, introverts have the opposite problem: they often feel burdened in environments where the stimulation comes from different sources.

7. You think of a vacation as productive time

8. To speak before 500 people is less stressful to you than you to talk to them in person later

9. In public transport, you prefer to sit on the edge of chairs, not in the middle

10. If you are very active, you start to lose energy fast

11. You would rather be an expert in one area but spread on more areas

12. You have a constant inner monologue

13. People have been calling you "old soul" since your 20s

14. People often tell you to get "out of your shell."

So, introversion represents a person's orientation toward his inner world in which he seeks stimulation and content that is emotionally satisfying and enriching. Introverted people are perceived as loners and those who do not like large groups of people and do not like to stay long within. Unlike them, extroverted people seek stimulation in the outside world, they are social, and it's easy for them to get in contact with new people.

According to scientists and psychiatrists introverts obtained theirs energy from individual activities, such as reading, fishing, walking, while extroverted prefer socializing and interacting with others. While the extroverts enjoy large and crowded places, the introverted person will tell you that it is psychologically tiring.

The fact is that some of the most important historical figures were introverts. I will list just a few: Gandhi, Edison, Leonardo da Vinci, Alfred Hitchcock, Albert Einstein ... Albert Einstein was even in the first years of schooling considered mentally retarded because he did not fit in the German schooling system which is largely based on extroversion. Until he moved to Italy, the young Albert had rotten grades, and he was even recommended to repeat the classes. Arriving in Italy, he met with a much different system of education that allowed individualism, and there's where Albert began to show the first signs of his genius. Painters, poets, and writers are largely introverted.

Writers in many cases transfer their introversion to their characters such are Sherlock Holmes, character of withdrawn mathematician from the movie "A Beautiful Mind" and Spielberg's Captain John Miller from the film "Saving Private Ryan" played by Tom Hanks. After all, how often do you hear that a writer loves crazy parties?

The big problem introverted people have is that today's culture is based on extroversion. Openness, expressed sociality and activity are considered good qualities. Today's society forces teamwork, which the introvert cannot handle because he achieves best results individually. People do not realize that introversion is a human trait, not a disease or disorder of any kind. Therefore, it is important to point it out to them because it will lead to easier understanding of introverted persons.

The assumption is that about 25% of the populations are introverts. Also, the problem occurs because teachers in schools are not familiar with this topic, and are unable to establish whether the child is introverted, or if a problem is something else. Children are placed under the category of "shy" and there ends any work with them. Introverted people, still have enormous potential because they can focus longer on a specific problem and to solve it much better than extroverted. While extroverted people give little importance to some things, introverts like to analyze deeply and to give it attention. Introverted people, in many cases have the ability to perceive the tiniest details.

"It's not that I'm so smart, it's just that I stay with problems longer." Albert Einstein

For introverted people is believed that they do not like to talk much, but that is not the true. They just do not like to talk if they do not have anything clever to say. I do not like to chat, but prefer topics that require deep thinking so I resent small talks that take away my precious energy. Ask me something that interests me and I can talk for hours. Also, introverts do not engage in conversation if they are not fully familiar with the matter. In this case, they only listen and absorb. Also, because they are not shy, introversion has nothing to do with modesty and these people have no fear of people, but simply do not like to be engaged in talks with everyone.

In the end, introverts are responsible for some of the greatest inventions in mankind because if were not for their introversion, the world would look completely different. Here is another official data that will help introverted people to more easily accept their connection to society and to be more secure in their abilities. The introversion increases with high IQ. Among the highly gifted people, there is a total of 75% of introverted people.

***

Introverted people just prefer to be alone, to spend time in solitude to preserve energy while time spent with other people can be very tiring and exhausting for them. They are preoccupied with the internal world: the world of thoughts, dreams, pictures and words. The need of an introverted person to be alone is not a sign of depression, but something that is necessary for them in order to regain their balance. I am a typical example of an introvert: I love silence, solitude, avoid crowds, meetings and everything that involves a large number of people. Although I'm introspective, I like to have long conversations while I do not like trivial stories and a waste of time (the phone is my biggest "enemy").

1. Introverts are very creative and a little (or a lot) eccentric. Some consider them to be strange, but I would like to call them (us) individualists.

2. Although they seem shy, they are brave enough to do public work, to help others and to share their thoughts and ideas with people.

3. They avoid conflicts, but when they speak out about something, you can be sure they stand firmly on their point of view.

4. They are not interested in superficial things.

5. Introverts like to talk, they just do not like banal chit-chat, and they prefer long, meaningful conversations.

6. Introverts are honest, and you can always have confidence in the honesty of their emotions.

7. Introverts are patient. Thanks to their ability to have fun even in solitude and to

get lost in their thoughts, it is easier for them to wait.

8. They never make important decisions in a hurry. They think about everything in details and are rarely impulsive.

9. Introverts do not like negative and emotionally draining people. Yes, they can be good friends and someone who "knows how to listen," but if you abuse their honesty, you will find they stop answering your calls.

10. When an introvert expresses his opinion or finally speaks about what bothered him for long, it shocks other people because of their belief that it is a shy person who cannot utter a bad word. Introverts sometimes keep their thinking to themselves for a long time, so they would not have to enter into conflict or hurt another person. When this happens, they do not look back.

11. Introverts can't become extroverts. If you want to get to know an introverted person, you should have a lot of patience. I have been told it took five years to get to know me.

Chapter 5:
The bad sides of being an introvert

1. They can be shy and reserved

It is very hard for them to open, and even when they try to suppress the shyness and be communicative, they are not relaxed and have the impression that their behavior is artificial, but not excessively. I often think about how others will experience me and how I would like others to see that I am a good person. On the other hand sometimes I think that maybe I am coming off as cold or not as nice as not okay some "popular" person. When I manage to open and behave relaxed, I simply remain without words. I think it's got everything to do with accepting myself as I am, but I didn't master it yet.

2. Introverts don't like the invasion of their "space"

That is, they do not feel comfortable when someone unknown or less known is sitting very close to them. Sometimes they are not comfortable when their friends and family are in their space. I do not think that is good, we should be more open towards other people's hugs and kisses.

3. Aversion to conflict□

Introverts often leave important conversations unfinished. Also, they should realize that other people do not read minds and that they must say what bothers them or what they want.□

4. Aversion to criticism

Especially young introverted people perceive any criticism of their conduct as an attack on themselves. My best advice is they should see things less personally.□

5. A strong need to receive praise and positive affirmations

This is my personal experience. So, no matter how outwardly indifferent to praise I might look, I feel very good when someone praises me.

6. They can react very emotionally to stressful situations

What is especially bad about this is that this reaction is often internal so reduces the sense of satisfaction in life.□

7. They have difficulties in abandoning the bad relationships

Since introverted people build deep relationships with other people, they find it difficult to quit them even though it turns out that they are not good for them. They always empathy for others, and often times put their personal feeling aside for them. □

8. They have difficulties when it is necessary to scold or punish others (for example children)

I believe that this is true, but I never felt I was doing something wrong if I didn't punish my children. □

9. They can be reserved when expressing their emotions

I consider this my greatest problem that brought me a lot of trouble in life, and emotional problems. So I advise all introverted people to do their best to express their feelings. □

10. They are often **perfectionists**; no one is perfect, and that is a trait of humanity.□

11. They tend to blame themselves for problems

As above, it is not a good feature, and it does not lead to a peaceful and contented life, and may have roots in the latent need to be substantial. □

Chapter 6:
How to raise an introverted child

Imagine this scene from everyday life. You are arriving to pick up your five-year son from a birthday party; his little friends are running and playing around. You are greeted by an unexpected sight: while other children are happily running around the yard with birthday boy, your son is in a corner of the yard in the company of the birthday boy's mother pampering the family dog, and he seems very happy. Or you come to kindergarten to pick up your daughter, and she is, instead of participating in group play, sitting alone in the corner of the room looking through a colorful picture book.☐

It is possible that these sights cause you anxiety, because you have a picture of your child as a highly social and open child (maybe even as a "leader of the pack"), or secretly believe that because of the enjoyment of such independent activities he is doomed to life full of sadness and loneliness. ☐

To "fix" the situation, you organize a social life for your child (in the form of everyday socializing, gaming, social activities), and you're wondering why he is nervous, tearful and upset. At the same time, from different parties you receive reliable information about how your child really enjoys having fun and playing with his close friend or cousins, and how he even more enjoys being in a small group of peers and without any problem fits in his kindergarten group. Is there really cause for concern? Answer: no, because you probably share your life with a child who could be characterized as introverted. □

Parents who love being in the spotlight often undermined the confidence of their introverted child trying to adapt them to their own values. The same goes for introverted parents who do not accept their introversion as they were feeling bad when they were kids so they do not want it for their children. From the children, we usually expect that they are happy, in a good mood and playful since "That is what children should be." Rarely do parents think that their nature may be different and that they also have the right to belong to extroverted or introverted personality type.

6.1 Why are we trying to make our introverted kid into an extrovert?

1. Mixing shyness and introversion

As I have already stated introversion and shyness are not the same. In fact, while the shy person avoids other people and in the background of such behavior is often a lack of confidence or fear of criticism, introverted do not care much what others think about their behavior. Hence the prejudices that introverted children and people are rowdy. However, they simply do not pay much attention to politeness since they don't consider it essential for a quality relationship.

2. General environment

The modern world has imposed certain ideals as a desirable value. Most adults believe that in this tough world those who are successful must know how to be proactive, which is the main motive for parents to try to change some features of their children. They have the best intentions, forgetting that their best intentions are sometimes not the best solutions for the child. □

Parents often use verbal violence and sneering to "wake up" their introverted child that is devastating. In this way, parents create an insurmountable gap in communication with their introverted child.☐

2. Is it possible to change an introverted child into extroverted?

Have you ever thought that the extroversion or introversion is actually inherited trait? Jerome Kagan, a developmental psychologist at Harvard, was dedicated to researching just introversion and in 1989 he performed an important experiment. By studying five hundred babies aged four months, he found that 20 percent of them are highly sensitive. The reactions have been observed about external events such as the burst of the bubble or the smell of alcohol. Kagan concluded that those babies tend to grow up to be introverted children, and then introverted adults. Years later, he found that toddlers who were highly sensitive in the early period "retain" those same responses as teenagers too. In this way, he confirmed his initial assumption that babies who were introverted at the age of four months remain with this feature even when they grow into teenagers. So the sooner you accept introversion of your child, it will be easier for both of you. □

3. Extroverted parents and introverted children

If one of the parents is an introvert, the child is usually introverted too, which contributes to a better understanding. However, when one or both of the parents are extroverted, the extroverted parent usually tries to make the child adapt to being extroverted too. In such cases, educators and child psychologists occupy a unique position, and recommend gentle guidance which includes: □

The true measure

For a child, it is important to feel welcome in the family, with the whole package of its characteristics, strengths and weaknesses. Never let him be under impression that he is not good enough to be accepted by you, because he doesn't meet your expectations. It will collapse his confidence, ruin your relationship and make him even more "closed" in himself. Instead, try to navigate, correct and encourage your child, but not beyond his personal capabilities, more in an appropriately dosed extent.

Encourage her in what is important to her□

Support "in the back" will further "open" your introverted child and strengthen her in the areas that you think are important. A child needs praise from parents regardless of whether it is "withdrawn" or "loud". Research shows that babies who were commended in the first year of life grow up to be optimistic people. Based on the initial impression of the baby that the world is mostly pleasant or unpleasant place, we can predict whether a baby will later in life become an optimist or a pessimist. If you meet your baby's needs, both physiological (feeding, dressing, bathing ...) and psychological (cooing, cuddling, embrace ...), you significantly influence on what kind of person it will grow up to be regardless of the classification into introverted and extroverted.□

Respect the nature of your child

Always respect the child's difference. Do not push him to be like you if you are extroverted, your child is entitled to his values, wishes, and ambitions. Keep in mind that your job as a parent is to direct, instead of trying to change the child's character.☐

Social contacts

The big concern, especially of extroverted parents, is that their introverted child will not have many friends. They think that the child with a reduced number of contacts will forever be lonely. If your child does not associate with a large number of peers, it also means that the relationships that it builds are much deeper and longer. After all, your child may not have 3,000 friends on Facebook, but would that be some evidence of success?☐

Support

Help him at an early age to cultivate relationships with peers by teaching him basic social characteristics, so he could satisfy his needs for a companionship with a small but select number of friends. It is your job to direct him towards the company and try to turn him on sports clubs or activities. It is your job to show him options and to support him, and he will find out what his interests are.

4. **For who is better that your child is an extrovert: for you or him?**☐

Prejudice

Introversion is neither diagnosis nor disorder. Introvert does not mean that your child is sad or condemned to a life without pleasures. ☐

Equal achievements

Numerous studies and experiments show that both extroverted and an introverted person can achieve the same academic success, if that is what concerns you as a parent.

Benefits

Introverts deeply reflect on the decision, which means they usually make the right decision, as I have already stated. They are successful in focusing on a specific problem, which contributes to the fact they come up with new, sometimes revolutionary ideas and solutions.

A sense of personal happiness

Finally, there are studies that show that introverted people often describe themselves as happy, and extroverted people see themselves as partially happy. Here's something to think about, especially those parents who suffer because their child is introverted. Is not a happy child what we all desire?

I think that the research show this because in an introverted person the feeling of happiness is based more on self-reliance while extroverts are constantly looking for some external stimulation. □

6.2 How to develop self-confidence and self-awareness in introverted children

Introvert children often wonder what and how to do things, think about who they are and ask themselves a lot of question. In this way, an image of oneself is created that can last a lifetime. By asking themselves these and other contemplative questions, the children seek answers to who they are and try to create an experience of the world, a way of communicating with the world and way to understand them better. It is true that introverted children are more sensitive than extroverted because they are constantly "in their head". No one says you have to act overprotective towards them, but you should bear in mind their can by hypersensitivity, which is not a bad trait.□

Children compare with each other in kindergarten, school, sports clubs, with friends and within different groups to which they belong and thus realize their values and abilities. Evaluation of themselves in relation to others brings them both positive and negative information about themselves so they know exactly what are their strengths, and what are their weakness. Self-confidence and self-awareness began to develop through 'self-evaluation.□

It is essential that we do not identify the terms self-confidence and self-awareness because they are different and do not have the same meaning, but are closely linked. It is important to distinguish these terms, but also to develop them in children.

Self-confidence is a measure of what we are capable of doing, at what we are good or bad, what we can and what we can't do and what are our capabilities and skills.

Self-awareness is the knowledge that we have about ourselves and experience of who we are, what we think of ourselves and how we can relate to that knowledge.

A child may be good at math, but not in the sport. The better child is at math; his confidence in this field is growing. However, that gives us a child that is good at math, but it does not mean it will help him to be good in basketball. Therefore, it is important that we develop healthy self-awareness and that the child knows to deal with their failures. The enhanced self-esteem of the child means that the child has a good self-image. Self-confidence is related to the child's achievement while the self-awareness is related to the child's existence. □

A parent can help the child develop self-confidence if the child is objectively praised for all his accomplishments and parents regularly give them feedback on his or her abilities and skills. A huge role in the development of self-esteem in a child, the parent has in helping him to develop a sense of competence. A large number of introverted children are often accompanied by an unrealistic sense of their capabilities; they think they are not capable or less capable than others and that even though they practice or train they will fail. Therefore, it is essential parental guidance in the right direction with support and encouragement.

Self-awareness can be seen as an internal pillar that we can keep stable, secure, "good in our own skin," but it can be unstable and then we feel guilty, unhappy and insecure.□

Why is the self-awareness essential?

A child who has a well-developed self-awareness is less vulnerable, has better relationships with other children and adults, is happier and enjoys life more. A parent needs to help the child to develop the quantitative and qualitative dimension of self-awareness.

Do we like company or solitude, do we like to speak in front of a large group or not, whether we are sensitive to injustice or we are not bothered by that. The qualitative dimension is the awareness of how we handle the facts we know about ourselves, in this way we will be able or not to separate the failures of us as individuals. This is very important because then the child will be able to say: "I got a bad grade because I did not learn, but that does not mean

I'm stupid and that I cannot learn that subject."☐

In developing self-confidence of the child, important reactions of parents to the child can usually go in two directions:

1. The direction in which we accept and respect our kid just the way it is with all its positive and negative sides.

2. The direction of insults, accusations and rejection because it is not the way we imagined it should be.

It is certain that the first line is the right choice to react to the child because it will allow him to develop a healthy and good self-esteem. If we accept both positive and negative sides of the child, the child will also accept and love himself just the way it is.

How can we recognize whether our introverted child has problems with self-confidence? The most common signs are:

1. The child is too quiet and shy

2. She is too self-critical and cries a lot☐

3. He shows a great distrust towards other people

4. She has a need to pamper other people

5. He apologizes for everything he did

6. She feels fear when trying something new and is too hard for her to make a decision or a choice. ☐

How can parents help?

Parents should by all means show their unconditional love, children need to feel and experience parents' love when they successfully deals with things, and when they are doing something wrong. ☐

Be honest with your child. Children always feel our honesty or dishonesty, especially those children who are more contemplative than others. What we are talking, must be seen also in our eyes, body, and voice. Look and listen to your child, talk to him "face to face" and really hear what he is telling you. Try more to understand his current situation and his feelings.

When you praise and when you criticize be specific, let your child know exactly what you mean, do not use some general phrases.

When criticizing, never criticize the personality of the child, just the behavior. e.g. "It is not right that you have taken your brother's things" instead of "You are bad". If your child is having trouble in school do not say "You have to begin to learn, you know you've got to fix it," but use a different approach, like, "I see that something is wrong, do you have problems in school? I wish you can tell me something about it. Can I help you? "When a child feels your sincere interest in him, he will turn to himself, reflect on and seek a solution to the new situation.

A parent should not only help a child to develop self-confidence and self-awareness but must show to his child by personal example how to love himself. Finally, it is important to say that parents should not forget that two-way education process, parents provide lessons to children, but also children give lessons to parents. Being a parent means that you need to enrich constantly and develop as a person. □

6.3 Whether your child is introverted or withdrawn for some other reasons?

Despite the fact that introversion in children is not considered to be an advantage, it isn't a disadvantage for the child. How will our children feel, largely depends on how we as parents treat their isolation. □

First of all we must understand that the introversion trait is not a disadvantage. Many people we know in whose company we feel comfortable are also introverted. Such people are often good "listeners" and peaceful people who are well adjusted in society. □

If your child's temperament is quiet and withdrawn, that is introverted, never say to other people things like, "He is withdrawn," especially if the child is nearby. It sounds a bit like an excuse, and that is not needed. □

There is nothing wrong in seclusion, on the contrary. Many people do not understand the reticence and think of it as a problem. They believe that the child suffers from a lack of confidence which is, in most cases, completely wrong and unfair to the child. Many withdrawn children have strong views about themselves, have an inner peace that shines and if open and "talkative" people could be quiet long enough they would see their luster.

Many parents are worried when a child runs away from a noisy crowd and raise the question of whether the child is just withdrawn or is there a problem that's bothering them? How to distinguish these two things? Observe your child when and how he communicates with others.

In fact, withdrawn child with a developed sense of self-confidence makes eye contact with other people in their vicinity and seems satisfied. Such children behave mostly polite, pleasant, and people feel good in their vicinity. □

Many withdrawn children are thoughtful and slower and more cautious in developing communication with strangers. They study a new person in their environment and question whether they are worth the effort of establishing a relationship. These children are careful in making friendships, but when they find a friend, it is usually a good and lasting friendship. Their reticence can be explained like aloofness and thoughtfulness, which are by no means negative traits.

Withdrawal as a reflection of internal problems

With some children reticence reflects their internal problems and such children are more than just quite. Such children are unsafe, avoid direct eye contact and have behavioral problems.

Other peers do not feel comfortable in their vicinity.

When you carefully observe such children, you will find that they are full of fear, uncertainty, and possibly anger. Instead of peace and trust, you will find in them unrest and distrust. If you notice this in your child's behavior, try to find out what causes such feelings and try to resolve it together.

Withdrawal as a mask

It is possible that some children hide behind the "retreat" in order not to allow the others to discover what they do not like in themselves. The label "seclusion" becomes an excuse for not developing their social skills and a reason to avoid the company of peers.

In these children, withdrawal is arising from an underdeveloped sense of self-esteem. Such a child has self-critical thoughts such as "I'm no good" or" I can do nothing well." Such a child is prone to become passive, very much withdrawn, or even depressed. When confronted with a new challenge, this child with low self-esteem will think, "I cannot do it."

If you notice that your child has a poor self-image and that it feels insecure, then you should in every way try to strengthen its self-confidence and self-esteem to help him to be equally involved in society. Such a child needs parents who can be trusted, on which he can always rely to treat him in a way that will diminish a sense of insecurity, frustration, and inner rage.

Puberty and behavioral changes

By entering puberty, many children become dissatisfied with themselves, uncertain and too self-critical. Before you tell your relatives for such behavior of your child, or consult a psychologist, be patient. Encourage your child and give him time to re-open to the world.

Parents often wonder what to do with the withdrawn child. Is this just a passing phase? Do you encourage your child to be more open? Is there a deeper problem?

Some more tips on how to behave if a child is withdrawn:

1. Acceptance

It is important to understand that you have a sensitive and withdrawn child who is slowly making contacts with strangers. ☐

2. Be careful what you say

If your child is withdrawn because she suffers from a lack of self-confidence and hasn't developed self-awareness yet, then make sure you do not hurt her with your words. Children are very sensitive to the words of their parents and important adults who they respect and value.□

Remember that a child should be praised for his efforts to carry out certain jobs, not only for the successful completion of the project. Take care not to exaggerate, or to speak untruth. For example, if the child did not achieve its goals, avoid sentences like "Next time you'll work harder, and you will certainly succeed." I would rather say something like "It did not turn out as you hoped, but I'm very proud of the effort you put into it."

Be spontaneous and full of love. Your love can certainly boost a child's confidence. Hold the child, kiss him, and show him how proud you are of him, not only because of his success but mostly because of who he is. Compliment him often and sincerely, but without exaggeration. Children have a great ability to sense when something comes "from the heart."□

You can't be a positive model to your child if you have low self-esteem because if you are self- critical, pessimistic, or unrealistic about your capabilities and limitations, there is a strong likelihood that your child will eventually "copy" or to develop a system of self-realization and behave in accordance with what he learned by watching and listening to you. Take care of yourself, as this will get your child a positive role, model.□

3. Don't force the support

We want to "help" to a withdrawn child, but usually this sort of endeavor has an opposite effect. It is much better to create a safe environment in which children can naturally develop their sociability.□

Never criticize your child because he is withdrawn and quiet and do not allow him to think that is something's wrong with that. If you are going to visit relatives, do not tell him in front of them not to be shy or explain him to them like "He/she is like that". It's much better before starting to explain to your child what behavior you expect from him, according to his capabilities.

When you are in a company and you notice that your child is feeling uncomfortable because the focus of attention is on him, try to move discreetly to another topic. □

4. Without pressure

Sometimes you wish that your withdrawn child demonstrates his talents and successes in front of your friends or relatives. Do not push him into the spotlight without warning. If you want your child to play some instrument or show any other talent in front of relatives or friends, ask him. Allow room for him to reject your wishes if discomfort is stronger than the desire to please you.

If your child is expecting a public appearance, help him overcome this skill gradually. If he plays some instrument, let him first make music in front of you or your closest friends.

5. Withdraw

Allow the child to express him and do not choke it with your eloquence. When someone asks something, do not answer for him. If you are talkative and extrovert, your child can be even more withdrawn in your company.

6.4 Are you overprotective toward your introverted child? □

Some parents are doing the same mistake in raising introverted children by being overprotective which in no case can be a good thing. If you are acting this way towards your introverted child you are not doing him a favor at all.

The basic postulate of every development, including child's, is defeating obstacles and challenges. As in adults, in children occurs sense of achievement after successfully mastering the challenges that give rise to confidence. We are all very aware that confidence is one of the basic requirements for success in any field of life. Problems in the development of the child's self-esteem arise whether when obstacles are insurmountable, or when a child does not have to overcome it. In a child who does not have any obstruction to overcome comes to a pathological personality development. We say these kids are overprotected by their parents or close family members. □

Overprotected child grows in the constant presence of two messages: that he is not capable and that this world is a very dangerous place. These messages form the idea of self, others, and the world, so instead of growing into an active and independent adult, it grows into a passive and dependent one. Passive because he does not dare doing anything out of fear he is incompetent, and that the world is very dangerous. The dependent because he is convinced that he cannot do it by himself so consequently he links to another person he expects to take care of him the same way his parents did.

If we ask why parents are overprotecting their kids when it gives poor results, the answer to this question is in the minds of parents. Overprotecting parents love their children as other parents do, but they are obsessed with fear and concern to preserve their kid's life and health. These parents do not distinguish love from the concerns and worries. □

Chapter 7:
How to make friendships

I suppose that most people think that friendships are made spontaneously. However, a few practical suggestions might help you to expand the circle of friends or strengthen friendships you already have☐

Friendships are, as we all know a very important part of life. For some people making friendships is a most natural thing, something that does not require effort. However, there are people who do not make friends easily. In childhood we all make friendships much easier, it's natural, but in adulthood for many of us this is not so simple.☐

Whether it is about introversion or poor social skills, it can prevent us to take the first step towards creating friendships. This section will give you practical suggestions that can help you enlarge the circle of friends or strengthen friendships that you already have. But it all starts with you. You must encourage yourself to move in that direction.

1. Prepare for friendship

The factors that you must consider are the following:☐

Attitude towards others

We can scare away potential friends with our behavior, by refusing compromises, and imposing our own attitudes, beliefs and behaviors. If you accept the fact that other people have the right to be different from you, you are open to new experiences and relationships that can enrich your life. Life would be boring if we were all the same.

Behavior towards others

Think about how you would like others to behave towards you and then behave the same way towards people in your life. So, if you expect kindness, honesty, and to be fully understood, you should offer these same qualities to potential friends. It may not be nice to say this, but when I was younger, I was very annoyed by extroverted people and their noise. The older I am, I become more aware that I have sinned judging people by how noisy or contemplative they are. From that point of view, there aren't only bias towards introverted by extroverted, but also vice versa.

2. Do not expect instant results

Good friends are not created overnight. Sharing the most intimate secrets on the same day you meet someone, does not necessarily create a close friendship. That kind of behavior can even repel that person. Do not force anything and let things just flow. Then after a while go with outsourcing and let your friendship hardened based on trust.

3. Harness the urge to criticize

Constant evaluating and criticizing of other people will distract them you from you in seconds. I do not mean just open criticism, but that inner one introverted people tend to do. You would not like anyone to start counting your faults.

4. Do not gossip

Although you might think that by gossiping you will keep the conversation flow, potential friends will not be able to trust you if you constantly comment on other people in your life. They'll think you will tell stories about them in the same way you tell about others.

5. Never underestimate and neglect yourself

Never underestimate you! Do not neglect yourself or restrict your opinion just to fit in socially.☐

6. Think what kind of friend you want☐

This is similar to when looking for a potential partner. Of course, everyone wants to find a friend who's sweet, considerate, and honest and has a good sense of humor. However, try to go a little deeper into the details: How would you like to spend time with this person? Do you need a shopping partner? Someone for a crazy night out or someone who will go with you to the exhibition or a museum? Maybe you need someone who shares same religious or spiritual beliefs as you are? In my life, I had and still have those with whom I can talk about spirituality and books and those extroverts to lead me to a party occasionally.

7. Where can you meet friends?

Now that we have solved the question of your needs and desires, it's time to find them. Where are friends hiding? In fact, at every step, you just have to be open to really want it.

Join a club or go to a course

Join a book club; take a foreign language course, yoga or some other course. Potential friends are everywhere, especially in places where people are connected by the same interests. To begin with, you automatically have at least one topic for conversation. After a conversation with someone, do not just go away, try to exchange numbers or email, or at least give yours. Do not immediately think that some person does not want you in their life if they did not ask you for a number, they are probably introverted. The most important thing is to listen to your feelings. If while chatting with someone you felt comfortable, it is most likely that the other person felt good too. Invite the person to coffee, it is no big deal. Perhaps this is the beginning of a beautiful friendship.

Volunteer

In every place, there is a voluntary association or nonprofit organization where any help is welcome. You will get to know a lot of people with similar interests, and, by the way, you will help those who need it. There is no better thing than that!

Go online

If you are reading this, it is obvious that you are already online and that you know how to use a computer, so why not try to make online friendships. And what is the best on the internet: these people do not have to be from your country so maybe one day soon, you will travel to some exotic country. I bet you have a Facebook account! □

Hang out with colleagues

Probably the easiest way to gain new friends is to hang out with the people you already spend time. If you are working in the same company or have a similar job, you already have something in common. Studies have shown that if you have at least one friend at work, it significantly reduces the level of stress and increases productivity. If you do not have much opportunity to spend time in the office, try to send a casual email to several "chosen ones" and invite them to lunch during a break or a drink after work. In the beginning be careful what you say, do not leap to the theme of your horrible boss immediately.

Go to your high school or college reunion ☐

This is something that many people avoid; however, anniversaries are a great way to reconnect with the people with whom you spent four or more years in the same school. You may renew that old friendship, but also make several new friendships. ☐

Get a dog

I not as a replacement for friends (although it definitely will become one, and no one will be as happy every time you return home, dogs are natural antidepressants). The fact is that dogs are magnets for people, and usually for nice people. Big chances are you'll meet other dog lovers. Whenever I walk my dog, I talk with at least with two dog lovers I meet.☐

Borrow friends from friends or relatives

This is actually a very effective method of finding new friends. Join the wider society of your brother or sister, cousin or a friend (if you want to expand the circle of friends) and try to find a soul mate. And what's best in the art of hunting friends is that someone close to you has already separated the wheat from the chaff.

Talk to strangers

This is the most extreme way to meet friends, but can be very effective for exploring. In fact, this way you can develop your courage. Remember the part in a book about making the first step. So, wherever you are, try to start a conversation with people: in the bookstore or a waiting room. When you expose yourself openly, the truth is that many times you will be rejected, but you may also meet your best friend or your guardian angel. I say this because I met one of my best friends in the toilets of a café during the afternoon coffee with colleagues from work. Every day is full of potential friendships: the waiting room, church, train, plane, building in which you work, cafe, library, gym...

8. **If you believe, however, that making friends is very difficult, here are some suggestions:**

I've already mentioned that you can easily plug in a course or a group where people share the same interests whether it's gardening or writing a story, so you'll at least have topics to talk about.

1. Observe and learn from the people who make friends easily.

2. Exercise to look people in the eye when you talk to them.

3. Smile.

4. See if there is someone like you in the room (who looks lonely and a bit lost) and then start a conversation with him.

5. When you talk to someone you've just met, ask them questions about

themselves: what they do, what they like to do in life, whether they have some hobbies, brothers or sisters ... This is a great way to make friends and introverted are known to be good listeners. □

6. Social skills, as I said can be learned, but to ask for help is not a disgrace. Contact a professional if you feel you need it.

9. How to keep a friendship?

Cherish your friends

Do not take friends for granted, no matter how long you were friends. Find time for them, and regularly let them know how much they mean to you. Friendships should be nurtured. If you are always busy and never have time to get together with them, why would they spend time with you? The same applies if you enter the relationship, or if you get a child. It is true that your life will change and you will no longer have much time for friends, but still find the time.

People make mistakes

Sometimes your friend will do something that might hurt you, but we are all flesh and blood, and nobody is immaculate. Provide support to friends, because you would like their understanding and forgiveness in case you do something wrong.

Check jealousy

You might want your best friend is to be faithful, which means that you, as in the love affair, feel jealousy sometimes. Refrain yourself from showing jealousy. Understand that love for friends is not the same as romantic love.

10. Avoid potential friends/enemies

As much as you are eager to make new friends, do not be tied down with people who you suspect might bring you more problems than happiness, no matter how lonely you are. No matter how fantastic potential friend looks, if he is passive aggressive, constantly criticizing and gossiping, it would be best to avoid him because in this situation things can only get worse.

7.1 How introverts and extroverts can be good friends

People differ in many ways, and it is hard to imagine that two fundamentally different people can be good friends. However, with a little extra effort and tips for better mutual understanding, friendships like mentioned ones are more than possible. It can provide us with a different view of the world and thereby enrich us as persons.

There are many personality traits, but most theories take into account the same basic characteristics. Among them are extroversion and introversion as a second polarity characteristic. These are, of course, two extreme examples. People may be more or less extroverted or introverted. But, as we have already established these personality traits have a big impact on our behavior and the choices we make in life.

Understand your introverted friend

You have to understand the silence and a desire for the solitude of your introverted friend. Introverts are often silent and often stay in their mind and forget that you asked them something. To better understand your introverted friends, take a moment to enter into their world. For instance, if you're at a party and they are quite and do not socialize much with other people, but tell you that they are having a great time, believe them. If your introverted friend says he is having fun, then he is, no matter what is your impression. Simply, you might have a different concept of fun and it is necessary for you to accept it. Also, if they leave early from parties or gatherings, they are not "Party breakers". They are simply tired of the fun since parties require more energy for them than for extroverts. □

When your introvert friend say to you he wants to spend some time alone on your suggestion about having fun; it is not because he doesn't like you. They simply need to spend some time alone and you should not take that personal. Extroverts are happiest when they are spending a lot of time socializing, but it's not the same with introverts. However, as I have already stated, they are neither lonely nor solitary types, but choose their company and will appreciate the friends who do not want to turn them into a sociable extrovert.

If an introverted person is sitting in the group remaining silent, that does not mean they condemn others. They are silent and listen to others and very probably they are having fun. Also, if you want to hear what they have to say, give them the time to say it and do not expect them to communicate in the same way as extroverts: fast and loud. Phone as a means of communication with your introverted friend cannot be an option because the conversation will mostly be one-sided. With an introvert is difficult to chat live, let alone over the phone. ☐

Understand your extroverted friend

Your extroverted friend is persistently trying to relax you to feel better in society and to interact with other people. He does not do that to make you upset although he can be very tiring. He's doing it in good faith. Extroverts often do not understand introversion and everything it means as long as you don't explain to them how introverts work and what are their needs related to society and socializing. Therefore, it is important to explain to your extrovert friend how the world looks through the eyes of an introvert.

If you are an introvert, extroverts may seem to you as they just talk and talk and in the flood of words, you are missing some higher meaning. But while extroverts talk much, it does not mean they speak nonsenses. It is necessary for you to have patience to listen to them and give them a chance to express themselves in their own specific way. Also, it is important to note that extrovert, as well as other people, do not read minds and you need to say what you think. □

At parties, extroverts can serve as a thrust engines for introverts what is mostly the case. Extroverts brought them up and slide, and the rest is to introverts. If we do not have extrovert friends, we would hardly ever go to a party. Extroverts are experts in chatting and meeting new people. They can be very useful in some business or family gatherings, especially when it comes to getting to know your partner's family. Introverts can, therefore, learn a lot from extroverts. On the other hand, giving life lessons in the mutual friendship between an introvert and extrovert is on mutual benefit, of course.

Finally, it is important to say that extroverts differ from one another. Likewise, and introverts differ. It is possible to find friends who are in relation to us and are in the second half of the continuum extroversion - introversion who are willing to adapt to us and teach us how to understand each other better.

Chapter 8:
You do not owe anybody explanations about your personal life

I know from personal experience that introverted people are more compelled to explain to others why they are doing something because they often feel that others do not understand or do not accept the way introverted act or behave. In the end, all these explanations are reduced to apologizing why we are who we are and in that way we lose a lot of our valuable energy. This was the case with me before I accepted what I am. Maybe this advice will not apply to all introverted people, but from my experience I believe that for many of them it will be supportive. Simply, although sometimes you feel it is necessary, some things you should never have to explain to other people.□

1. You do not owe anybody an explanation of your life□

Whether you decide to live with a roommate, alone, or out of wedlock   you do not have to explain to others why you have made such a decision. Believe me, it's so liberating when you realize that you don't need to explain or to justify yourself to others.□

2. You do not owe anybody an explanation for your life priorities

Want to take a break in the studies and during this period do the traveling or planning to open your own business, and put the personal life aside? Your priorities are only yours, and you don't need to justify yourself for that. Those who love you will understand and support you whatever you decide because those people know that you need those things.□

3. You do not owe anybody an apology if you're not sorry

If you did something that the other person does not like, and you are not sorry about it, you should never apologize. The apology is an attempt to correct the mistakes and the impact it has had on other people. If you think you are not wrong and you are not sorry, do not ever apologize. We often apologize even though we know that we are right, and that isn't good, especially not for our self-esteem.

4. You do not owe anybody an explanation for the time you want spend alone

If you want to be alone, that does not mean that you are unfriendly or rude. You simply need to dedicate some time just for yourself. You can tell to close people in your life that you need to be alone, that's all, do not ever justify yourself to others why you need solitude. Enjoy this time dedicated only to you.

5. You do not owe anybody an explanation about your religious or political convictions and beliefs

When people share with you some of their beliefs, it's usually a sign that they have confidence in you. But just because someone shared with you his thinking, it does not mean you have to be in agreement with. Each of us has an opinion about everything in our environment, and because

we are friends does not mean we have to agree on everything. ☐

6. You do not owe anyone to say "YES" to whatever they say

I know it's hard sometimes to refuse people, especially some that are much more demanding and pushy, but you should know your limits. If you are unable or for any reason you do not want to do something then do not. And do not worry about that, nor spend much time explaining your acts to others. Say what you have and be done with that, respect your time.

7. You do not owe anybody an explanation for your physical appearance

If you've lost weight, gained weight, grew a beard, changed hairstyle, put piercings or done something else with your physical appearance, you don't have to justify yourself to anybody. □

8. Never explain why you prefer some food to the other

Everyone likes a different type of food; some prefer meat and sausages while others are more in fish and seafood. If someone is "bothered" that you will, in the restaurant where steaks are a specialty, order grilled calamari, who cares! □

9. You do not owe anybody an explanation about your sex life

Whether you have an active sex life, or you're in a causal relationship, it does not need to concern anyone except yourself. People will try to condemn you because of your sexual orientation and decisions with whom you sleep, but it is not really their thing. Never let someone bothering you because you are alone or in a "socially unacceptable" relationship, it is your life and live it how you want. I'm not saying that we should not accept advice from some well-meaning person, but the only parameter is how much you are actually happy in your love affair.

10. You should never explain to anyone why you are alone

Many people find that having a partner and be in a love relationship is the only thing that is important in life. Of course, it's nice to have someone beside you, but if you are alone, it is not the end of the world. Whether you have just broken a relationship and do not want to jump immediately into another, or you may have careers now as a priority and simply do not want to get involved in some emotional stories again, it's your thing. □

11. You do not owe anybody an explanation of your valid decisions regarding marriage and children

If you have agreed with your partner that you will live out of wedlock, you will not have children or maybe you do not plan marriage and children, the environment should not be given any justification. Your life, your stuff!

Chapter 9:
Learn the skills of flirting

Flirting is a way to meet potential partners and to see whether they are compatible with you. In some situations, such as going out or partying, flirting is the only way to open the door for an emotional relationship with someone you do not know, and who you might, otherwise never see again. Because of all this, flirting is a very important skill, and it is something that makes many people nervous, introverted people maybe a little more. There is a whole art of flirting, but it is an art that can be learned. Here are a few tips that can be helpful.☐

Instruction

1. Do not expect too much

Flirting can be fun, but only if you don't take it too seriously. You can flirt with someone briefly and then it can happen that you never ever again speak to that person, but that's flirting. If you always get into flirting with some huge expectation that you will start dating or even marry to that person, you will be very disappointed and you'll probably seem a little desperate, and the results of flirting will rarely be positive. Do not forget, you are just flirting. □

2. Read the body language

Does the person you are flirting with seem approachable or interested in you? From the moment you see the person with whom you wish to flirt, start by reading his / her body language. When you start flirting with that person, body language is often the only way to see whether the person is interested in you. Most of us are naturally gifted to read body language, but the signals can easily be misinterpreted, so be careful and patient. If you see a signal which indicates that the person is interested in you, wait for the other signals who will confirm that. □

3. Get eye contact, but briefly

The most important thing is not to stare because it's really disturbing for the person you're staring especially if she herself is introverted by nature. Make a cursory glance at the person, smile a bit, and then slowly look away. If you look back and notice that the person is looking in your direction, he/she is probably interested in flirting with you.

4. Start a conversation with the person you are interested in

It is important to react quickly after a successful flirting by starting a conversation. If you do not know the person, you are flirting from before and then just chat though you probably do not like it, but you cannot immediately discuss your life philosophy with a stranger. Perhaps the best way to start the conversation is by starting with a simple observation which ends with the question: "It's a nice day, is not it?" Or "This place is crawling with people?" These are just some examples; I believe that you will come up with something better. It does not matter what you say; you actually need an ask this question to start a conversation with someone if that person wants it. If the person politely replies, continue the conversation. If the person does not respond, or if it looks busily or not interested, then he or she probably is not interested in flirting with you. At the beginning of the conversation is not advisable to talk about anything personal. Talk about your environment, the play that you recently saw, etc., but do not talk a lot about yourself and do not ask personal questions. □

5. Gradually reveal information about yourself, according to the system of reciprocity

If the chat goes well, keep it up by discovering a little something about yourself, like, what you do for living or how you liked the show you watched. Of course, at some point you will want to say your name in hope that you will hear the name of a person you are flirting with. The key to sharing information is that you are both gradually opening to one another. Talk to one another in shifts, and every time he or she shares some information about themselves, you can say something about yourself, and you can say a little more than that. For example, if you talk to a girl who says she is attending some classes during the summer, maybe you will discover that you're doing the same. This is an invitation for her to disclose more information about herself. In this way, the intimacy of the conversation gradually increases. However, do not reveal too much about yourself in a short time, and neither ask the person you are flirting too many questions. Also, do not just be silent and listen without talking about yourself if you're wishing to stay in touch with someone.□

6. Always give undivided attention to the person

Laugh at her/his jokes, listen to her/his story, and do not divert your attention to what is happening around you. It is more important to act interested but to be an interesting person all the time. Careful listening is far more important to successful flirting than ingenuity, which again is a gift of introverted people. ☐

7. Use body language to suggest your romantic intentions

If the situation is going well, try to overcome the barrier of touch; but not in the first 5 minutes, if you know what I mean. During the conversation, you can gently tap his or her hand at one moment. Or, be confident and when crossing the road, keep him or her by the arm, or if you go to your table in the restaurant, gently lead the person with whom you are by holding his hand. Such contact helps to break down the barriers of "personal space". Pay attention to red flags, because some people have problems with the "personal space", and you don't want to put them in an awkward situation. Many women feel threatened when the man they just met enters their personal space while most men are more accessible to the touch. In any case, proceed with caution, and back away if you get negative or mixed signals.

8. "Close the deal" ☐

Mostly harmless flirting is fun, and it will in most situations finish in just flirting. But from time to time, you will meet someone you would like to see again and who you think would like to see you again. After all, flirting is a kind of courtship ritual, a way to meet a potential boyfriend or girlfriend, maybe even a future spouse. But as I already stated, never in the beginning think so much about the future or even worry about the wedding plans; start by taking the phone number. For most people, this part is difficult because in fact they have to disclose their intentions and run the risk that they will be rejected. Be courageous, because you have nothing to lose. Tell the person that you want to see them again and just ask for a phone number, or, if it seems right, try to schedule a meeting in the near future. If a person is not interested, do not worry. There will always be some guy or girl, with whom you can flirt. ☐

Advice

1. It is not particularly important what you say at the beginning of courting but whatever you say, try to make a casual conversation.☐

2. The first time you talk to someone relax as much as you can. This will make you both feel less pressure and chances for success will be much higher.☐

3. If you are embarrassed to ask for a phone number, try to give your number. If the person you are flirting is really interested in you, he/she will call. However, I don't recommend that you do this with an introverted female person as she probably will not call you first even if she likes you.

4. While flirting with someone, do not pick up your cell phone because it shows that you are interesting to talk to someone who is not present or just hiding in some way behind the mobile phone.☐

5. As for breaking the barriers of contact with a girl, try the proven way. For

example, offer her hand when she needs help to maintain balance when entering or exiting the car, or when she needs to jump over an obstacle or some uneven surface. Girls love this because it shows that you care about them, and not just about yourself. This is very desirable if she is elegantly dressed or wearing high heels. If the situation is more casual, go somewhere where she will have to step on something high (like platform or wall). Go first, then turn around and hold her hand to help her climb. How does she react when you offer her hand? Was she happy to accept it, or in a hurry to release your hand? □

Warnings

1. Do not flirt with someone in who you are not interested to be your potential partner, unless you are 100% sure that neither he/she is not interested in you, because then there is a risk that he/she might be hurt. □

2. Flirt in a way that matches the atmosphere. The meeting in the library or a club with loud music, for example,

might not be suitable for too much of the story. In this case, you will have to adopt by acting interested and wait for a spontaneous opportunity to meet in the hallway or at the bar. But do not follow a person around because you are too nervous to approach her; if you do, you will act as a weirdo. Talk to this person as soon as you get a first chance.

3. Flirting is not suitable everywhere. Funerals, for example, are not in any way a good place to flirt. A place where you work is also inadequate, but if it, however, happens, behave decently and do not overdo it, if the other party is not interested.

4. Although humor is a good way to flirt, try not joking too much if the person you are flirting looks uncomfortable. While rude jokes often come to mind during the flirting, some people are just not comfortable with it and it can lead to rejection, or may lead to an uneasy silence that would spoil the mood and because of that you will feel uncomfortable yourself. Think before you speak and remember: you do not have to be funny all the time,

and each person has a different definition of humor.

5. Do not complain while flirting. Remember that the world does not revolve around you. If you complain too much, others will get the impression that you are depressed and avoid you. This also applies to the constant belittling you, which is not the same as modesty; moreover, it is a form of self-centeredness. It is normal if you occasionally feel bad and show your discontent, but you must also know when to get over it and move on. □

Chapter 10:
Is the solitude your choice or the consequence

We must ask ourselves whether and how is solitude good for us, although we regularly find it among introverted people. Sometimes, I believe it is in bad taste when we speak of them/us as if we are some foreign species. It is true that an introverted person cannot become an extrovert, but is the label of introvert a justification for inaction or laziness. So in this chapter I decided to find out the good and bad sides of seclusion and loneliness and to try to introduce a variety of causes of solitude. Not all of them are the consequence of introversion.

Solitude in the sense of being alone can represent the need for space and time in which a man is devoted to him with positive connotations and is not necessarily pronounced with negative overtones. The man is a social being but also has the need to "be" with himself. Each of us should have some time alone when we make choices, decisions, or we are working on ourselves. As much as the interaction with people is of crucial importance for human development, it is important to have some time alone for developing self-awareness and self-development.

The quality of both will be clearly reflected in our personality.☐

But when in being alone we find the basis for all further problems, inconvenience, and dissatisfaction in life; if it crystallizes our labiality and destroys our confidence, then we have a completely new context.

Solitude as a choice from all bad reasons

This one, I think, is one of the most dangerous things that can happen to a man. A person who lives alone and consider that to be the best option for her life, the person looks relaxed and happy in first months of her solitude. However, if such a person isn't working on anything to improve their life or the quality of her solitude, then the passage of time causes dissatisfaction in terms of personal feelings of underachievement. It also causes doubts in everything and everyone and a sense of bewilderment which will rapidly decline the level of self- confidence.☐

All these and other similar things can perform exactly from the solitude or irrational attitude towards the same. Often such life forms develop in the pathological picture of severe depression because one starts to justify everything through his desire for solitude, without realizing his contribution to the existing emptiness. The strength of one person can be viewed through the prism of lifestyle that the person leads. The personality that is stable and rich in spirit draws from his solitude energy for tomorrow, and never disturbs his balance.

Solitude as the consequence

Solitude as the consequence is a common life picture, usually associated with a sense of loss of loved ones, that is when the person is all alone in the physical sense. In such a situation, one cannot escape the impression that the force of destiny, some higher power of all powers, brought him to a state of loneliness without his will. If a person is stable, she will process loneliness in a rational way and will not see it as the end of the world. Life goes on; these forms of solitude leave their mark on the personality but are not "unworkable". Each person will find their way to express it. □

The problem becomes more serious when it comes to being alone because of the loss of a life partner, parent, or any person who they were attached to or in some way dependent. The fact that this relationship of dependency is interrupted can lead to a very dangerous state of mind of the person who remains in seclusion.

There is no longer a bare solitude, first arises the feeling of disorientation, then meaninglessness and loneliness. Then we can talk about loneliness as a consequence, whose outcome will depend on whether a person will become aware that it can and should fight for their place in the world. □

Is the solitude a good choice for you?

Solitude can be a very common option for introverted people. When a person chooses solitude, she is rather convinced of the correctness of her opinions. The reasons for this sort of solitude is quite logical, and usually the thought is other people opinions seems to be less valuable. If a person's solitude is his choice, sometimes it is possible that it is a specific consequence of bad experiences with people, whether in business, whether on personal.□

A feature of this loneliness is a conviction of the person that her choice is the correct one, and that is the chosen way of life. However, because of this conviction, such a person doesn't experience her solitude as a burden. On the contrary, she made this choice consciously, knowing how to deal with all that solitude implies. They build a box for themselves, living space they develop in detail, and almost none of them will consider they are living in solitude, but that it is the way others sees things.

This choice has to be acknowledged. But the question is how much can a person get from her solitude. ☐

Giving and receiving is something that fulfills a man, and what ultimately makes the man. Before you make your choice, it is desirable that you respond to some hypothetical questions. The choice of solitude can be a healthy thing with the real perception of things around you and deep and continuous work on yourself, but it canclose you off to the outside world.☐

Solitude can be enriched with self-discovery. I can enjoy my lifestyle but others would call it "solitude". They have their reasons for their choices as I do, however, my choices are not a danger neither for me, nor for my environment, and they don't include isolation.

Attention should be paid to the solitude in those radical forms, from which it is logical to expect some negative consequences. Each indicator to suggest that you move from "safe" solitude in this "potentially dangerous" one is a call for you to think twice about how truly happy you are alone. Such forms of solitude and loneliness are what a man should be afraid of. And if this is so, then keep your eyes and heart open, clear your mind and put the strings of life back in your hands.□

Chapter 11:
Introversion and love relationships

Love is the process

The transition from "me" to "we" requires a change in perspective in terms of that it is required to invest a certain energy which is very important for introverted people to know. True partnership is a development process.

It isn't difficult to enter into a marriage or partnership, but creating true community is a difficult task. This task can be achieved only with respect to the development and creation of a healthy relationship in which we will continuously invest time, attention and patience necessary to comply. We must not allow acceleration to disrupt the natural flow of love and development. Many people amazed with the idea of love do not allow time to judge whether a certain person and relationship is right for them.

Phases of love

1. Connecting

Connecting occurs when an exchange between the two people flows without restraint. The beginning is often initiated by a mutual physical attraction. Sometimes two people who know each other for a long time reveal that there is something more than comradeship in their relationship and get into a love affair. However, the first case is more common, and the initial attraction is the main motivator for a mutual relationship and convergence. □

2. Testing

The testing phase is characterized by endless discussions on key experiences and events in their lives and the need to know more about a potential love partner. This is the phase of gathering information, and introverted people should not withhold information about themselves as a potential partner can be very frustrating. □

People should use this phase to learn more, ask questions and listen carefully to the answers. Pay attention to what the other person said at the start. Ask around about your partners past. Where did he grow up? Where did he go to school? What kind of childhood did he have? Who and what are his friends? Does he has brothers and sisters, and what is their relationship? Why did he choose this profession? All this will help you to get a complete picture of the person. It is especially important to pay attention how he/she acts in relation to you. Does he interrupt you when you speak? Whether it's easy for him to say "thank you" or not? Does he offer you to try what he eats? Does he call when he says he will? □

Ask him about his hopes and dreams that is what he wants for himself, what is most important in life for him and what are his objectives. At the same time, the partner will discover everything about you. Be careful not to seduce someone with misrepresentation to believe that you are different from what you are. As a rule, impersonation naturally prevents binding to a deeper level. Ask tough questions related to a personal philosophy of life. Feel free to ask questions that may be sensitive and delicate, do not just nod your head. □

3. Evaluation

Suppose that you and your partner have successfully crossed the stage of research and decided to go further: then you enter into what might be called a phase in which love "builds or destroys" -Phase of assessment or evaluation. Now weigh the pros and cons information and determine whether it is worth investing in that relationship. This may all sound too analytical, maybe even repulsive, but building strong connections requires the presence of your rational mind in the midst of splendor and beauty of your turbulent emotions. It is not easy to "assess" partner when you are amazed at everything he does. The most important thing in the choice of a romantic partner is the right criteria. Many people choose partners on the basis of something that is changeable and transient like appearance, sexual attraction, sexual ability, money, work, etc. and then they realize that their relationship breaks down when one of these benefits disappear. If a relationship is based on shared activities or hobbies, and one day they end, then what is left? □

4. Building Intimacy

On this level of pulling your relationship deeper below the surface begins the formation of "We". Intimacy is built through deepening your original connection. In fact, an intimacy means a certain degree in which "I allow you to get inside my world." It is the degree to which a person allows another person to approach her in the emotional sense. The intimacy allows you to know what the other person feels and when he or she isn't expressing their feelings. To connect separate realities, you have to know what your partner is experiencing, and vice versa. It takes you to share the hidden thoughts, feelings, joys, fears, dreams, worry, sadness and pleasure to build ties of intimacy. Think of these links as fishing strings that are stretched from one person to another. The more strings you set, the relationship gets stronger. For you to entwine many strong strings, strong enough to build a bridge between two of yours separate realities, takes time.

5. Giving promise or commitment

Giving promise means that you shifted from "I think I want this relationship" to "I know I want this relationship." This is the moment when you go from uncertainty to the security and from hesitation to action. Commitment means that you will put "all the eggs in one basket". To make a love relationship go in this direction, both partners should commit themselves and surrender. If one person commits and the other does not, the relationship can withstand imbalance only a short period before it slides into displeasure. Some people are very afraid of commitment. Before you can truly enter a new relationship, you should look at the mistakes of the previous and heal your wounds. This is something that each person must do for himself. The only thing that a partner can do is to make a safe for the other partner to expose his fears and anxiety and be patient until he is ready for commitment, but even a commitment requires a certain degree of risk. Nothing in life is with a guaranteed outcome.

If you enter into a marriage make an agreement about your relationship, first of all, you should specify how both of you should behave and interact. This agreement will be the glue that will hold the two of you together when disagreements or circumstances threaten to separate you. Find a right time to negotiate an agreement. If you talk about it too late, you can already acquire the habits and behaviors that are difficult to change.

The optimal time to create an agreement is soon after you are committed to each other and your relationship. It would not be bad that these agreements are on paper so you could be periodically reminded. Although the word contract can be scary, do not let that deter you from making one. Sit down and talk about what is the common objective of your community and what is the purpose of your marriage. What are you going to be to one another and how will you nurture your relationship?

Then you can determine the basic rules of how you relate to each other. For example: "We agree that we listen to each otherconfession. We talk to each other when something is bothering us. We care about each other when we are sick ... "I think for introverted people are especially important to understand the importance of communication in love or marital relationship. It is particularly important to emphasize in the contract how you will talk to each other when there is a disagreement. For example: "We agree not to interrupt each other and not to leave home when we are angry. We agree not to insult one another. This will make the disagreements in the future less unpleasant. In the end, agree how you will keep up with the ups and downs that life can bring. How will you fight together when something traumatic happens? How will you celebrate successes and happy events? Life can be like a roller coaster, and these agreements may serve as seat belts. When you arrange and build agreement in writing, you should both sign it and leave it in a safe place. Every year you should look at it again and revise, if necessary. ☐

Also, make agreements on the roles and responsibilities. They relate to questions such as: Who handles the finances, cooks dinner, takes out the trash; who fixes things when they break down, walks the dog, plans entertainment, organizes vacations, etc. Determining roles and responsibilities may seem like a job, but if no one knows their responsible, things will fail. This makes it possible for the building process to develop consciously and naturally and thereby increases the chances to create a strong and lasting foundation that will stand the test of time.

Most problems manifested in relationships can be reduced to three essential: fear, control and limit.

Fear

Fear is a lack of confidence, and trust between the partners is necessary. It is imperative for you to consider and release the fears you have regarding your partner so you could create a relationship without doubt and restraint. □

In relationships, often develop fears associated with the notion of intimacy. Being in a relationship means that you allow someone to get close enough to you, but also to maintain a certain distance to preserve the personal identity. To learn to maintain and enjoy the right balance of closeness and distance is a significant task. Fear of abandonment and its opposite: the fear of capture is the most common reason for the problem of trust in love relationships. If abandonment is your problem, you may find yourself in a relationship that is bad. If you are constantly in anticipation that your partner will leave you, you can react in two ways: either to firmly tie a partner or to leave first in order not to be left behind. In both cases, your expectations will be fulfilled. □

If your problem is fear of capture, you will feel stifled whenever a person comes too close to you. Fear of bonding, contrary to the abandonment, is the fear that you will never get enough space because the other person is too suffocating. The lesson for fear of entrapment is to overcome panic and indeed remain, even when you feel you are suffocating.

Control

If one partner is a person who is prone to control, he or she cannot participate in the process of give and take, which is necessary for a real relationship, since he or she will always have a need to determine how the things should be done. Control prevents "we" to completely develop. The partner who is inclined to control always takes the lead, making plans, deciding when and how they will be together, and in the marriage he takes all decisions by himself. If control is your problem, you will need to release your inflexibility because your partner will surely at some point feel bad about it because he has no power. "I know best" and "I do not have to ask" will certainly lead to the collapse of the relationship.

Borders

Maintaining boundaries is a major problem for many people. Borders define the scope of who you are and what you are and what you are not willing to do. When you engage in a romantic relationship, this division can become blurred. The mist leads to confusion as to where one person stops and where the other begins. If you have a problem of boundaries that can be shown in your stewardship and servility. We can call that sort of person "a person who cannot say no". People can easily get used to imply that such a person will always do them a favor and will quickly lose their sense of proportion. Everything begins to be the default, but a partner that was used secretly feels dissatisfaction. It is necessary to state clearly what you want and what you don't want and to protect and defend yourself. No man can't read minds, as I have repeatedly stated, so it is necessary to express what you feel or think loudly and clearly.

5 lessons to learn

Your relationship is a "non-school" that teaches you how to work with each other while you are in the process of bonding. You learn by experimenting with different methods until you find one that is effective. There are basic lessons that we must know when we engage in a love relationship. Among them are sharing, patience, gratitude, acceptance, and forgiveness. In the course of your relationship, situations will appear that will require you to apply these lessons.

Sharing

Without sharing, a partnership is a clear association of two people who look only after themselves. Sharing is the essence of teamwork and partnership. Sharing refers to your body, emotions, thoughts, time, space and personal belongings.

Patience

Patience is a virtue useful in life and in love. Each person moves, develops and progresses in line with its own pace and rhythm. The partnership requires you respecting the dynamics of the other person, either in the physical, emotional, intellectual and spiritual sphere.

Gratitude

Your relationship will require you to learn a lesson of gratitude to make sure you never see your partner as something that goes without saying. Learning to appreciate your partner in terms of everything that he is and that he does will strengthen your relationship with him.

Acceptance

Acceptance means that you appreciate qualities of your partner and accept his shortcomings and the way he lives and works. Every loving couple has to deal with differences. The basis for dealing with these differences raises the basic willingness to accept your partner exactly as he is. How can you accept those things that irritate you, annoy you or even make you angry? The answer is by providing your partner understanding and acceptance as you want for yourself. The partner is an individual for himself, and it isn't his only aim to make you happy. If something bothers you, just imagine how you would feel if he or she expressed animosity towards you.

Forgiveness

When two people form a bond assuming that is based on trust, and that trust is violated, it takes great strength and effort for forgiveness. Depending on the severity of the treachery, assess whether you can forgive and forget or forgive allegedly. In this case, it is better to end the relationship, but to transform it into sadomasochism. So remind yourself of your contract and, if the error is too significant to overcome, end the relationship. If you feel that you can understand partner and identify with him, forgive him and do not ever come back to that. This refers to the significant flaws that involve violation of the basic agreement (the refusal of communication, lies and adultery).

Chapter 12:
Introverts and career

Best jobs for introverts

Introverted people have great powers of observation; they are great listeners and pay attention to detail and are therefore by default meant for some jobs. If someone often takes a back seat and just listen and observes and not participates in the conversation and jokes, does not mean he is boring. Introverted people pay more attention to detail and are often better organized than extroverted. And precisely because of these advantages, they are great for the following jobs:

1. Astronomer

Take the footsteps of the great scientists as Galileo, Copernicus, and Newton and insert in this well-paid work studying the stars or work with satellites. And only the sky will be the limit.

2. Expert in communication in social networks

Although it sounds very ironic, account/profile management of a company on Facebook, Twitter or another social network, can be the perfect job for an introvert. It's a job that requires a lot of time spent on the computer and just the small amount of time in real communication with people.

3. Criminalistics sociologists

Criminalistics sociologists are specialized in finding the cause, correct, and prevent crime. Typical activities include independent analysis of criminal behavior, study how the use of police techniques and new legislation affects the crime rate and report writing.

4. The court recorder

This job is mostly limited to the conduct of transcription during court proceedings, and the interaction with others is kept to a minimum.

5. Graphic Designer☐

Silent types can express their creativity by designing logos, websites or any other things. Graphic designers are more inclined to independent work. They arrange the deal with the client, but then they retreat and do their job alone.

6. Financial Analyst

Thanks to their natural, innate accuracy, introverted people are born for this job that requires constant analysis, the 'behavior' of shares and bonds, the study of business trends and writing financial statements. Financial analysts are very focused on the numbers and it is a solitary job.☐

7. Translator

Since they are more prone to listening than talking, introverted people by nature have developed an ear for languages. That is why they should invest in foreign language learning and engage in a fast-growing business area of translating written documents from one language to another.

8. Writer

Because of all the properties listed in this book, such as analytical skills, attention to detail and introspection, introverted people are often very talented at writing, either creatively or some other sort of writing.

Tips for introverted entrepreneurs

Entrepreneurs are usually associated with extroversion but introverted people have advantages that they can use when communicating. According to most studies, a minimum of one-third of the population is introverted. However, people who do not like to be the center of attention can be very successful entrepreneurs; they just need to know their character and virtues.

Many of introverted entrepreneur leave the spotlight and media attention to its talented workers since they prefer to work in peace and quiet.

1. Learn to work with what you have

No matter how much your palms are sweating at the thought of talking with customers, as an entrepreneur you are doomed to communicate and it cannot be avoided. Of course, this does not mean that you have to put yourself in awkward situations that you find unbearable. If you feel uncomfortable talking in front of a large audience, organize meetings with clients in person, and it will usually be sufficient for the establishment of cooperation; or apply the advice from this book on public speaking. If, however, you can in no way avoid speaking in front of a larger audience, be sure to prepare notes. Identify your strengths and weaknesses and adjust them. Successful independent entrepreneurs learn to overcome their weaknesses and to promote their qualities.

2. Prepare for work outside the comfort zone

Introverted entrepreneurs enjoy spending time alone with their thoughts, but entrepreneur cannot completely avoid interaction with customers and associates. Getting around in interpersonal relationships is essential for recruiting quality employees, recruiting investors and even to sell your ideas. So, you can be introverted most of the time but reconcile with a fact that sometimes you will have to be social.

3. Be aware of your energy

We have detected that you will occasionally have to put on a mask of sociality to accomplish some goals. In order to ease the processes always prepare. For example, if you absolutely have to call someone regarding some project, do it when you are calm and ready. A good principle is that you first perform the tasks that require extroversion, while you still have energy, and not later in the day. □

5. Technology never feels uncomfortable

We live in a digital age that provides many benefits to the introverted people. Inconvenience can be avoided with just a few mouse clicks. Social networks, e-mails, and various applications can save you a large number of stressful situations and so use them wisely.

There are many ways to communicate with people indirectly, and when you feel you do not want to talk, you can delegate extroverted associates, and you should not forget the possibility of the famous "outsourcing" that will definitely limit your personal contact with workers.

Finally, be aware that even technology cannot solve all the problems just as well as the character is not the same thing as destiny. Be wise, calm, and build a system that will make your life easier. Nothing in the business world is that hard as it looks at the beginning.

How to fight for your place at work

If you are an introverted person, it is likely that your colleagues have characterized as "feeble" and "scared". However, there are introverted people at every workplace. Contrary to popular belief, introverted people are not necessarily inactive. Moreover, most of them are brilliant. They accumulate their energy from within. You may not often hear them in meetings but you'll be delighted with their presentations, the effect on the business and results. □

Introverted vs. extroverted people

It is true that extroverted people are more appreciated in work, regardless of whether they are good at what they do. This is something that can hurt or irritate many introverted people. However, most of them do not care about this situation, because they find refuge in their circle of people, in their behavior and way of doing business. □

Introverted people, as I have already said, are not necessary shy. They simply are not too loud and like to draw energy from their inner world. Although they put a lot of effort, introverted people find it quite difficult to survive in office, given that extroverted people prevail and are constantly looking for attention with the way they talk, their style, enthusiasm, and approachability.□

Excellent business performance

The best weapon of an introverted person is a passion which can be seen throughout their business performance. If you are an introverted person, then, to prove yourself, let your work speak for you. It's okay that you do not like to be the center of attention, but then make sure that you do the work that is impeccable. Any good employer will recognize the quality and, if you are committed to work, you will ensure yourself one of the top places in the office, and you will be respected for the quality of your work.□

Great observation of the business situation

Although introversion is often characterized as a negative thing, a lot of introverted people have brilliant ideas. Introverted people often have a sharp memory and are great for troubleshooting. Introverted people are often bright monitors of the situation (as opposed to extroverted people). They are also often well prepared to cope with unforeseen events. Introverted people are looking to build long and stable business relationships.□

Put yourself once at the forefront

If you are introverted, does not mean that you should reject the recognition that you deserve for your severe and hard work. Everybody needs some recognition. If you carried a heavy project to an end, praise yourself a bit, even in a subtle way. You are maybe not the most interesting person to drink coffee during the breaks, but do not let your hard work and dedication remain on the fringe because you think it does not really matters. □

Introverts can be great leaders

Psychologists point out that the advantages of introverted leaders in relation to extroverted are many. They listen better; they do not need to be the center of every conversation, have the knowledge and do not rely on the charm. When we think of leaders, usually we hold in our head image of a charismatic, communicative and confident person. But introverted people are great leaders, as evidenced by cases of computer genius, billionaire Bill Gates, Warren Buffett and Barack Obama. □

Psychologists point out that the benefits of introverted versus extroverted leaders are many. They do not need to be the focus of every conversation and is not a problem for them to wait until every person in the room presents their ideas to get scored with their own at the end. They do not rely on charm and ability to draw from an awkward situation but are well prepared for everything. While most people remain on the surface, they can delve into the matter; they know how to ask the right questions, listen to the answer and to separate the extraneous details. ☐

One of their biggest advantages is the ability to stay focused, even in the moments when the rest are scattered. They have a soothing effect on the environment, which is especially important in times of crisis through which every company goes. They act calmly when things are going well, rather than to "fly" on the wings of success they are self-critical and aware.

And finally, they write more. Although we live in the age of modern technology, old-fashioned writing is still important because it leads to clear thinking and good communication.

4 Tips for shy girls

I noticed a lot of introverted young girls whom their job matters, but do not know how to fit in and often lose their jobs or remain on the fringe.

So I decided to write and 4 tips that I think will help them to express themselves at work and retain employment.

If you are a shy and discreet girl, it will be harder for you to reach business success. So I suggest a few ways to overcome your inhibitions, discover your personal abilities to superiors and display yourself in the right light.

Improve your speech

Do not let your ideas and statements sound like a question. To gain the proper authoritative voice, practice at home. □

Talk in numbers, not adjectives

Introverted people do not like boasting and exaggeration and "showing" around, but if your superior isn't informed of your potential, work, results, and if you don't impose it to him, you're done. However, there is a way to showcase your achievements in an acceptable way. If you are asked whether you will finish the job on time, answer it will be done two hours earlier. Do not speak that you will, for example, achieve "super sale on the ground", but say that "sales will be 20 percent higher."

Contact your boss for help

In a subtle way ask for help and advice from the boss, for example, the question can be: "Is there a better way to do this job?" So you will not have to talk in front of everyone, which will result in a more relaxed atmosphere. It will draw attention to your ideas and you will immediately get feedback on what the presumed thoughts about your work are.

Invest in appearance

Your appearance says something about you before you open your mouth, so invest in your wardrobe. Ignore the dark, gray and earth colors. Choose attractive pieces, gentle, cheerful colors, put a wide belt or an interesting necklace. Let it be your practice every day. Simply stand up for your place under the sun! □

Conclusion

Thank you again for downloading this book!

I hope this book was able to help you to clear some dilemmas and questions you probably had about introverted people whether you are yourself an introvert or someone close to you is.

If this book has helped in any way to feel better, to start working on your self-esteem or to understand a bit more yourself, your introverted friends, children or partner, then this book met my goal and I'm very pleased about that. And finally to get back to basics and remind you that before you can change yourself you have to accept yourself completely as you are.

Finally, if you enjoyed this book, then I'd like to ask you for a favor, would you be kind enough to leave a review for this book on Amazon? It'd be greatly appreciated!

Thank you and good luck!

Printed in Great Britain
by Amazon